Table of Conter

MW00934680

3

Common Core
State Standards

Third Grade Workbook
STUDENT EDITION

Grade 3

- **Math Standards**
- **English Standards**

Worksheets that teach every Common Core Standard!

<u>Stripes</u>

<u>Directions:</u> Read the passage below about Stripes. Answer the questions about the text. Ask your own questions that can be answered by reading the text.

Stripes likes to hang out in the bushes eating bugs and little plants. But, Stripes is always alone. He is friendly and can't understand why creatures always scurry away when he is around. They don't even give him the chance to say hello. As soon as they see Stripes, they do their best to look elsewhere and get away as fast as they can. Stripes feels lonely and confused.

He wonders if it has anything to do with his looks. Stripes is not the cutest guy around, but he tries his best to keep his fur neat and clean. The white stripe going down his back is always bright and shiny. Stripes is kind and would love to help out if anyone would let him. He really wants to play with someone. He feels he needs to come up with a plan to find out why so many creatures avoid him.

<u>Answer these questions about the text.</u>

1. Who is the main character in this story? What kind of creature is he? How do you know?

_____

_____

_____

2. What does Stripes look like?

_____

_____

3. What is the problem Stripes has?

_____

_____

<u>Ask two questions about this text.</u>

_____

_____

_____

Standard: Reading l Literature l RL.3.1   ©http://CoreCommonStandards.com

Name: _____

Glow Stick

Directions: Read the passage below about the glow stick. Answer the questions about the text. Ask your own questions that can be answered by reading the text.

One day at his uncle's, Carter was hoeing the field when the hoe hit a glowing stick. He picked it up and examined it and put it in his pocket. An hour later he was planting the corn, wheat, and soy seeds. His back hurt. "I wish these things would plant themselves" he thought. He turned to get more seeds, but they were gone! Carter whipped around and saw that all the seeds were already in the ground.

He looked at the strange stick and whispered, "I wish the plants would grow fast and tall." Carter looked up in awe and saw a sea of green sprouts.

The next morning, a shadow loomed over Carter's window. He looked out and almost fainted. Where the field used to be, a forest stood. Carter grabbed the stick and ran outside. Carter's family was amazed. Cousin Bud was grabbing the chainsaw to start harvesting. But Carter was worried. What if the plants kept growing and fell on the house? He was determined to un-wish this catastrophe.

That night, while everyone was asleep, Carter ventured into the forest of wheat, corn, and soy and wished the crops would return to normal, and that his family would forget the whole day's occurrence. When he awoke the next morning Carter was happy to see a field again with newly sewn seeds. Bud was getting ready to water the seeds and Carter's uncle was sitting down for breakfast. The last thing Carter did before joining his uncle was to go out behind the barn and bury the stick deep in the earth.

Answer these questions about the text.

1. Where does this story take place? How do you know?

_____

2. List the parts of the story that are realistic. List what parts are fantasy.

_____

_____

_____

3. Why do you think Carter buried the stick back underground?

_____

_____

Ask two questions about this text.

_____

_____

_____

ICARUS AND DAEDALUS

by: Josephine Preston Peabody (1874-1922)

The following short story is reprinted from *Old Greek Folk Stories Told Anew*. Josephine Preston Peabody. Boston: Houghton Mifflin, 1897.

Among all those mortals who grew so wise that they learned the secrets of the gods, none was more cunning than Daedalus.

He once built, for King Minos of Crete, a wonderful Labyrinth of winding ways so cunningly tangled up and twisted around that, once inside, you could never find your way out again without a magic clue. But the king's favor veered with the wind, and one day he had his master architect imprisoned in a tower. Daedalus managed to escape from his cell; but it seemed impossible to leave the island, since every ship that came or went was well guarded by order of the king.

At length, watching the sea-gulls in the air,--the only creatures that were sure of liberty,--he thought of a plan for himself and his young son Icarus, who was captive with him.

Little by little, he gathered a store of feathers great and small. He fastened these together with thread, moulded them in with wax, and so fashioned two great wings like those of a bird. When they were done, Daedalus fitted them to his own shoulders, and after one or two efforts, he found that by waving his arms he could winnow the air and cleave it, as a swimmer does the sea. He held himself aloft, wavered this way and that with the wind, and at last, like a great fledgling, he learned to fly.

Without delay, he fell to work on a pair of wings for the boy Icarus, and taught him carefully how to use them, bidding him beware of rash adventures among the stars. "Remember," said the father, "never to fly very low or very high, for the fogs about the earth would weigh you down, but the blaze of the sun will surely melt your feathers apart if you go too near."

For Icarus, these cautions went in at one ear and out by the other. Who could remember to be careful when he was to fly for the first time? Are birds careful? Not they! And not an idea remained in the boy's head but the one joy of escape.

The day came, and the fair wind that was to set them free. The father bird put on his wings, and, while the light urged them to be gone, he waited to see that all was well with Icarus, for the two could not fly hand in hand. Up they rose, the boy after his father. The hateful ground of Crete sank beneath them; and the country folk, who caught a glimpse of them when they were high above the tree-tops, took it for a vision of the gods,--Apollo, perhaps, with Cupid after him.

At first there was a terror in the joy. The wide vacancy of the air dazed them,--a glance downward made their brains reel. But when a great wind filled their wings, and Icarus felt himself sustained, like a halcyon-bird in the hollow of a wave, like a child uplifted by his mother, he forgot everything in the world but joy. He forgot Crete and the other islands that he had passed over: he saw but vaguely that winged thing in the distance before him that was his father Daedalus. He longed for one draught of flight to quench the thirst of his captivity: he stretched out his arms to the sky and made towards the highest heavens.

Alas for him! Warmer and warmer grew the air. Those arms, that had seemed to uphold him, relaxed. His wings wavered, drooped. He fluttered his young hands vainly,--he was falling,--and in that terror he remembered. The heat of the sun had melted the wax from his wings; the feathers were falling, one by one, like snowflakes; and there was none to help.

He fell like a leaf tossed down the wind, down, down, with one cry that overtook Daedalus far away. When he returned, and sought high and low for the poor boy, he saw nothing but the bird-like feathers afloat on the water, and he knew that Icarus was drowned.

The nearest island he named Icaria, in memory of the child; but he, in heavy grief, went to the temple of Apollo in Sicily, and there hung up his wings as an offering. Never again did he attempt to fly.

Standard: Reading I Literature I RL.3.2

Name: _____

Icarus and Daedalus

Directions: Read The Greek Mythology Tale *Icarus and Daedalus.*
Answer the questions and think about the moral of the story.

Answer these questions about the text.

1. Who imprisons Daedalus?

_____

2. Where does Daedalus get the idea for his escape?

_____

3. Who is Icarus?

_____

4. What did Daedalus warn Icarus about?

_____

_____

5. What happened to Icarus?

_____

_____

6. What is the message that can be learned from reading *Icarus and Daedalus*?

Use details from the story to support your answer.

_____

_____

_____

_____

_____

Standard: Reading l Literature l RL.3.2   ©http://CommonCoreStandards.com

The Tortoise and the Hare

The hare was once boasting of his speed before the other animals. "I have never yet been beaten," said he, "when I put forth my full speed. I challenge anyone here to race with me."

The tortoise said quietly, "I accept your challenge."

"That is a good joke," said the hare. "I could dance around you all the way."

"Keep your boasting until you've beaten," answered the tortoise. "Shall we race?"

So a course was fixed and a start was made. The hare darted almost out of sight at once, but soon stopped and, to show his contempt for the tortoise, lay down to have a nap. The tortoise plodded on and plodded on, and when the hare awoke from his nap, he saw the tortoise nearing the finish line, and he could not catch up in time to save the race.

Slow and steady wins the race.

Name: _____

The Tortoise and the Hare

Directions: Read *The Tortoise and the Hare*.
Answer the questions and think about the moral of the story.

Answer these questions about the text.

1. Who was bragging at the beginning of the race?

_____

2. Which animal got to the front position right away?

_____

3. What did the tortoise mean when he said, "Keep your boasting until you've beaten" ?

_____

4. Why did the hare take a nap?

_____

_____

5. Who won the race?

_____

_____

6. What is the message that can be learned from reading *The Tortoise and the Hare*?

Use details from the story to support your answer

_____

_____

_____

_____

_____

Standard: Reading l Literature l RL.3.2   ©http://CommonCoreStandards.com

Name: _____

The Character

Directions: Choose a character from a story. Describe the character at the beginning and end of the story and the events that occurred that helped to cause any change.

Story: _____ Author: _____	**Character Change**	Character Name: _____ Character Drawing:

In the beginning:

In the end:

Events that happen in the story that may have caused a change in the character.

Name: _____

Know the Character

<u>Directions:</u> Choose a character from a story. Write something in each bubble that describes the character. Think about the character's feelings, traits, thoughts, and physical appearance.

Story:

_____

Author:

_____

Character Name:

_____

Character Drawing:

Write about something the character does that effects an event in the story.

Standard: Reading | Literature | RL.3.3   ©http://CoreCommonStandards.com

Reading Nonliteral Language

Directions: Read the story provided. Find examples of nonliteral, or figurative, language used within the story. Write the examples, then rewrite them in literal language. Make sure the meaning stays the same.

Story Title_____

Author: _____

Examples of Nonliteral Language	**Examples Rewritten in Literal Language**

Name: _____

Percy and Sally

Directions: Read the passage below about Percy and Sally. Identify the examples of nonliteral language, {such as metaphors, similes, personification, and onomatopoeia}, and write them below.

Percy and his sister, Sally, were bored out of their minds because the weatherman said it was going to rain cats and dogs. The sky turned as black as coal, and the wind whistled. But after that crazy storm, it was as dry as a bone. So Percy and Sally swam in the pool. While they were swimming, the ladder fell and Percy had to reach over and pick it up. "You are as strong as an ox," said Sally. Percy just winked, cool as a cucumber. Sally was a fish in the water, swimming all day. Splash, splash, splash. Percy sat on the grass and began to build a rock tower and was as busy as a bee. A gentle breeze came and the flowers danced in the wind. It was a perfect summer day.

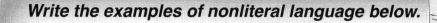

Write the examples of nonliteral language below.

©http://CoreCommonStandards.com

Name: _____

Drama, Poems, Stories

Directions: Label the following examples correctly with STORY, DRAMA, or POEM. Write whether the example shown is a *stanza*, *chapter*, or *scene*.

Which type of writing does
this text represent?

_____

Which type of writing does
this text represent?

_____

MR. FORD: That is one fine-looking motor car you have there sir. CARL: Why thank you. I just received   it. It was ordered over a year ago ad was delivered yesterday. MR. FORD: A year? To wait for a car? That seems like an awfully long time. CARL: Well, that's how long these things take. What can you do. *Mr. Ford thought about that. What could he do to improve production of the new automobile?* *Ford exits stage left.*

This is an example of a

_____

yellow chickens clucking fast fluffy white sheep bleating past cows are mooing, kitties mew horses neigh and love doves coo animals on henry's farm in the barn now nice and warm sleeping 'til the morning light barn owls watch them overnight

This is an example of a

_____

Which type of writing does
this text represent?

_____

Captain Roberto yelled from the bridge up to the crow's nest, "Do ye see any ships on the horizon?" There was no answer. The Captain pointed to his first mate and out Carlos ran to the deck and up the mast to the crow's nest. Looking down, Carlos had a face of utter confusion. No one was in the nest. Where did the two men go? The Captain and his first mate themselves saw the men ascend. Immediately, a large, black crow flew overhead. A crow? What was a crow doing 50 miles out from the shore?

This is an example of a

_____

Standard: Reading I Literature I RL.3.5

©http://CoreCommonStandards.com

Name: _____

Robert Frost

Directions: Read the poem *Stopping By Woods on a Snowy Evening,* by Robert Frost. Robert Frost wrote this poem in 1923 while he lived in New Hampshire.

Read each of the four stanzas and discuss what the words mean. Read each line of each stanza, picturing what the narrator is describing.
How do the stanzas create a structure for the poem? Would the poem make sense if the stanzas were in a different order?

Use these questions to guide you.

Who is the narrator? _____

What makes you think this? _____

In stanza I, where is the narrator? _____

_____

What makes you think this? _____

In stanza II, how is the setting further described?_____

_____

In stanza III, describe the sounds the narrator hears. How does this further illustrate the setting?

_____

_____

_____

In stanza IV, what do you think the traveler means when he says, *And miles to go before I sleep*?

_____

_____

_____

How do you feel about this poem? _____

_____

_____

Standard: Reading I Literature I RL.3.5   ©http://CoreCommonStandards.com

Name: _____

What Kind of Story?

Directions: Match the book cover to the type of story it is. (genre)

poem

story

fantasy

non-fiction

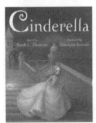

photo-essay

mythology

history

realistic fiction

play

mystery

fable

fairy tale

Standard: Reading | Literature | RL.3.5

Name: _____

Small Things Add Up
Story By: Andrew Frinkle

Olivia was walking along the sidewalk on the way home with her friend Victoria. As they walked, Victoria saw something shiny. She kicked at it with her feet and sent it bouncing along.

Ting! Ting! Ting!

The shiny thing skipped across the pavement. Victoria smiled and kept walking. Victoria liked to bounce balls, skip stones, or kick things. The sound made Olivia curious, so she stopped to look.

"Hey, it's a penny!" Olivia said excitedly. She bent down to get the coin.

"So? Those things are worthless. I have a whole bunch sitting in the bottom of my sock drawer." Victoria watched with amusement as her friend picked up the coin.

"I don't mind. They add up if you get enough of them."

"It takes a hundred of them to make a dollar, and a dollar isn't even worth much. Besides, they smell funny, too."

"I like the way they make my finger smell when I handle a lot of them. It makes me feel rich." Olivia grinned.

"You're weird."

"I always stop to pick up coins, especially silver-colored ones. I get about a dollar a month for free by doing it. That's more than ten dollars a year to buy things with!"

"I won't pick up anything less than a quarter. It's annoying."

Olivia shook her head. Her friend was fun, but sometimes she whined too much. Free money was free money. All she had to do was pick it up. "If you don't want them, pick them up and give them to me instead."

"Maybe." Victoria shrugged.

As they continued to walk along, they came across another coin. This one was a nickel. Victoria stopped and looked at it.

"Are you going to get it?" Olivia asked.

Victoria thought about it. "You made me think I need to start collecting free money, too."

Olivia remembered what her grandfather always said: "If you don't take it when it's offered, it won't be there when you need it."

"You're pretty smart. I think you deserve this more than me." Victoria handed over the nickel. "Thanks." Olivia smiled. "I'm saving up for your birthday present anyway."

Victoria smiled at her friend and kept an eye out for more coins as they walked the rest of the way home. It became their thing.

Standard: Reading I Literature I RL.3.6

©http://CoreCommonStandards.com

Name: _____

Small Things Add Up

Directions: Read the story on page 2, *Small Things Add Up*. Choose one of the characters. Think about how your point of view differs from that character's.

Character's Name

_____

Character's Point of View on topic (Picking up coins off ground.)

_____

_____

_____

_____

My point of view on topic. (Picking up coins off ground.)

_____

_____

_____

_____

Why I feel this way.

_____

_____

_____

_____

Standard: Reading I Literature I RL.3.6

Name: _____

Inside the Game
Story By: Andrew Frinkle

Jason tapped his fingers quickly on the buttons of his controller. Just one more boss and he'd reach a new level! His tongue was hanging out of his mouth and his eyes were stretched wide open as he made his character jump and dodge and attack.

Ding-Dong!

"Jason, honey? Can you answer the door?"

"I'm busy, mom!" Jason shouted back at his mother. Couldn't she see how important this was? He'd spent three hours so far working to this point in the game. He *couldn't* stop now.

Ding-Dong! Mom's footsteps approached the front door.

"Jason, it's your friend Todd." Mom called from the doorway.

Todd, his best friend, stepped into the room. "Jason! Let's go shoot some hoops. I need a partner for a pick-up game down the street." He sounded exited.

Jason snorted. "No way, Todd. I'm playing a game here." Couldn't anyone see how busy he was? What was wrong with people?

Todd shook his head. "Look, you can kill that boss later. Let's go."

Jason gave his friend a dirty look, and his character almost got killed while he looked away. He quickly used another potion in his game. "I almost died because of you!"

Todd looked at Jason's mother. Jason's mother looked back at him. They both looked at Jason. "Why don't you go play some basketball with your friend?" Jason's mother suggested.

"Tomorrow, maybe…" There were more levels to beat tomorrow, though. Maybe he'd go play tomorrow. He'd have to see what mood he was in. He thought he heard footsteps walking away, but he was too busy beating the next level to care.

An hour later, Jason's father came home. It was dinner time after father washed up and sat down. Jason didn't even hear his name being called to the table. He didn't hear father walk up behind him and ask him to turn the game off, either.

When the screen suddenly went black and father's angry face loomed in front of him, Jason finally heard. "No more game for a month." Jason's father growled at him. "You don't play basketball, you don't come to dinner, and you don't do your chores. We'll make sure everything else gets done before you play anymore."

Jason nodded slowly. He knew better than to argue with his father, and when he thought about it, he had been playing quite a bit. It was fun, but he was letting down his friends, his family, and himself by playing too much.

He'd try harder in the future.

Name: _____

Inside the Game

Directions: Read the story on page 2, *Inside the Game*. Choose one of the characters. Think about how your point of view differs from that character's.

Character's Name

_____

Character's Point of View on topic (Playing video games)

_____

_____

_____

_____

_____

My point of view on topic. (Playing video games.)

_____

_____

_____

_____

_____

Why I feel this way.

_____

_____

_____

_____

Standard: Reading I Literature I RL.3.6   ©http://CoreCommonStandards.com

Illustrations

Directions: Choose a story. Draw one illustration from the story. Think about why the illustrator drew that picture. Write or talk about how that illustration helps to tell the story.

The book I chose is

_____

Here is an illustration from the book.

What can you tell about this illustration? How does it help to tell the story? What mood does it create? How does it enhance the characters or setting?

Name: _____

Mythological Illustrations

Directions: Read *The Tales from The Odyssey: One-Eyed Giant*, by Mary Pope Osborne. Draw one illustration from the story. Think about why the illustrator drew that picture. Write or talk about how that illustration helps to tell the story.

Here is an illustration from the story.

What can you tell about this illustration? How does it help to tell the story? What mood does it create? How does it enhance the characters or setting?

_____
_____
_____
_____
_____
_____
_____
_____
_____
_____
_____
_____
_____
_____
_____
_____
_____
_____

Standard: Reading I Literature I RL.3.7   ©http://CoreCommonStandards.com

Level: Third Grade

Name: _____

Identifying Theme

The Theme is what the story teaches the readers. Themes are related to the real world.
Themes are inferred, or implied, by the reader as they read the story.

Directions: Read two stories with similar themes and compare the stories.

Story One		
Main Characters		Setting
Problem		Solution
What is the theme of this story? What happens in the story to make you think this?		

Story Two		
Main Characters		Setting
Problem		Solution
What is the theme of this story? What happens in the story to make you think this?		

Standard: Reading I Literature I RL.3.9

©http://CoreCommonStandards.com

Name: _____

Comparing Stories with the Same Author

Book Title: _____   Author: _____   Book Title: _____

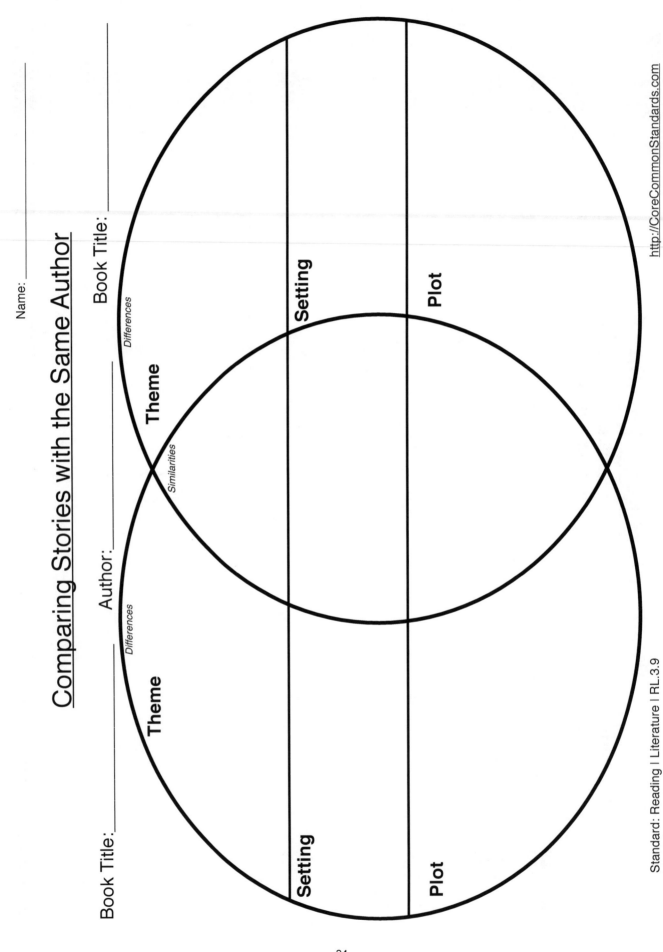

Theme

Differences

Setting

Plot

Similarities

Theme

Differences

Setting

Plot

Standard: Reading I Literature I RL.3.9

http://CoreCommonStandards.com

Name: _____

Identifying Theme

The Theme is what the story teaches the readers. Themes are related to the real world. Themes are inferred, or implied, by the reader as they read the story.

Directions: Read four similar stories from four different genres. Complete the chart for each story and identify a common theme for all.

Genre Title	non-fiction _____	fiction _____	poem _____	biography _____
characters				
conflicts				
events				
theme				
common theme to all				

Name: _____

What I Am Reading

Directions: Keep track of the stories you read this year in Third Grade. When you finish a book, write the title and the date you completed the book. Did you like the book?

Date	Book Title	Did You Like the Book?

Standard: Reading I Literature I RL.3.10

Level: Third Grade   Name: _____

What Are They Reading?

Directions: Keep track of the stories your students can read this year at grade level. Write the date each genre was read successfully.

Name	non-fiction story	realistic fiction story	fantasy story	informational story	poetry

Standard: Reading I Literature I RL.3.10   ©http://CoreCommonStandards.com

Name: _____

Crayfish

Directions: Read the passage below about crayfish. Answer the questions about the text. Ask your own questions that can be answered by reading the text.

The crayfish, also known as crawfish or crawdad, is found in fresh water that will not freeze completely to the bottom. Like their lobster cousins who live in salt water, crayfish breathe through gills. The crayfish is a decapod crustacean and has twenty body segments grouped into two body parts; the cephalothorax (head and thorax) and the abdomen. Two pairs of antennae, one long, one short, can be found on the head. Two, large pincer-claws and four pairs of legs are also found extending from the cephalothorax. The abdomen is made up of six ring-like segments, four of which have short appendages that are used for swimming.

Crayfish usually grow to about 17 cm (7 in) and can be found in varying colors, such as white, red, brown, orange, or green. They hatch from eggs and the young look very much like the adults, except they are smaller. It takes several years for a crayfish to reach adult size, and as they grow, their outer shell sheds and a new one takes its place.

Crayfish live in fresh water at the bottom of lakes and streams. They crawl along at night in the mud eating worms, insects, mollusks, and decayed plants and animals. The large claws are used to crush and tear food into smaller pieces. If the crayfish is threatened, these claws act as a defense, lifted high, as the fan-shaped tail pushes the crayfish backwards kicking up mud at its predator.

Answer these questions about the text.

1. What is this main idea of this passage?

_____

2. What is a way crayfish and lobsters are alike? Different?

_____

_____

3. Explain the uses of the crayfish's pincer-claws.

_____

_____

Ask two questions about this text.

_____

_____

_____

_____

Standard: Reading I Informational Text I RI.3.1   ©http://CoreCommonStandards.com

Name: _____

Mount Rushmore

Directions: Read the passage below about Mount Rushmore. Answer the questions about the text. Then, ask your own questions that can be answered by reading the text.

Mount Rushmore was created between 1927 and 1941. It was sculpted by Gutzon Borglum, who was 60 years old, and 400 other workers. The purpose behind this magnificent landmark was to stand as a memorial to this country's birth and ideals. It is a symbol of a great nation due to great leaders. Mount Rushmore is located in the Black Hills of South Dakota.

Four Presidents are sculpted into the 5,725 foot mountain: George Washington, Thomas Jefferson, Theodore Roosevelt, and Abraham Lincoln. Washington was selected because he is the father of our country. Jefferson was chosen since he was the author of the Declaration of Independence and responsible for the Louisiana Purchase. Roosevelt has his face on the monument for the completion of the Panama Canal and his contribution to National Parks. And finally, Lincoln was selected to be on Mount Rushmore for preserving the union throughout the Civil War.

It took 14 years to complete and, at the time, $1 million. Each president's face is as tall as the entire Great Sphinx of Egypt, or 60 feet from chin to top of the head. The noses are 20 feet long, each mouth 18 feet wide, and the eyes are 11 feet across. You can visit Mount Rushmore to learn more about its history and view its grandeur yourself.

Answer these questions about the text.

1. Why was Mount Rushmore sculpted?

_____

2. Whose faces are on Mount Rushmore?

_____

3. Describe some details about Mount Rushmore.

_____

_____

Ask two questions about this text.

_____

_____

_____

_____

Standard: Reading I Informational Text I RI.3.1   ©http://CoreCommonStandards.com

Name: _____

John Orozco

Directions: Read the passage below about John Orozco. What is the main idea of the text? Recount the details and explain how they support the main idea.

John Orozco is a dedicated, hard-working Olympic gymnast from New York. He is the youngest of 5 children of Puerto Rican parents, William and Damaris. John began gymnastics when his dad saw a flier for free lessons in Manhattan. John became so talented, his mom drove him 30 miles from his home in the Bronx to Chappaqua for his practices.

John hurt his achilles in 2010 during a competition. It was a tough time for John, but his family and friends encouraged him not to give up. After he graduated from high school, John focused all his time on training for the 2012 Olympics.

At the 2012 Olympics, John came in 8th place and did not get to stand on the podium. But he was proud of what he accomplished and is looking forward to competing in the 2016 Olympics in Rio de Janeiro.

_____
main idea

Key Detail and how it supports the main idea.

_____

_____

_____

_____

Key Detail and how it supports the main idea.

_____

_____

_____

_____

Key Detail and how it supports the main idea.

_____

_____

_____

_____

Standard: Reading I Informational Text I RI.3.2
Graphics (c) DailyHerald.com

©http://CoreCommonStandards.com

Name: _____

Edamame

Directions: Read the passage below about edamame. What is the main idea of the text? Recount the details and explain how they support the main idea.

Edamame is the new, healthy snack! Edamame is a green vegetable, also known as a soybean, that are picked before they ripen. The name edamame, in Japanese, means twig bean, and is appropriate as the beans are harvested with their twigs still on. Evidence suggests that edamame has been used since 1275 and is rich in carbohydrates, protein, dietary fiber, and other nutrients.

Edamame began as a common cuisine in Japan, China, and Hawaii. The pods are boiled in water with salt, or other spices, and served whole. Sometimes they are streamed. Another way of serving edamame is by puréeing them and making a dip for crackers or other vegetables. Edamame is quickly becoming a favorite tasty and very healthy snack.

_____

main idea

Key Detail and how it supports the main idea.

_____

_____

_____

_____

Key Detail and how it supports the main idea.

_____

_____

_____

_____

Key Detail and how it supports the main idea.

_____

_____

_____

_____

Standard: Reading I Informational Text I RI.3.2
Graphics (c)fedebelle.com

©http://CoreCommonStandards.com

Name: _____

Order of Events

Directions: With a partner, read some text of a science experiment or a historical selection. Write 4 key events from the selection onto the cards below. Cut out the cards and trade with your partner. Have your partner place your cards into the correct order and write summary of the events using time order words. You do the same for your partner's cards.

Story: _____

Author: _____

Summarize the events using time order words.

_____

_____

_____

_____

_____

_____

_____

_____

_____

_____

Event	Event

Event	Event

Standard: Reading I Informational Text I RI.3.3   ©http://CoreCommonStandards.com

Level: Third Grade   Name: _____

How Events are Related

Directions: When reading informational text, be aware of the relationship between the events that take place. One event may cause the effect of another. Record such events on the graphic organizer below.

Story: _____

Author: _____

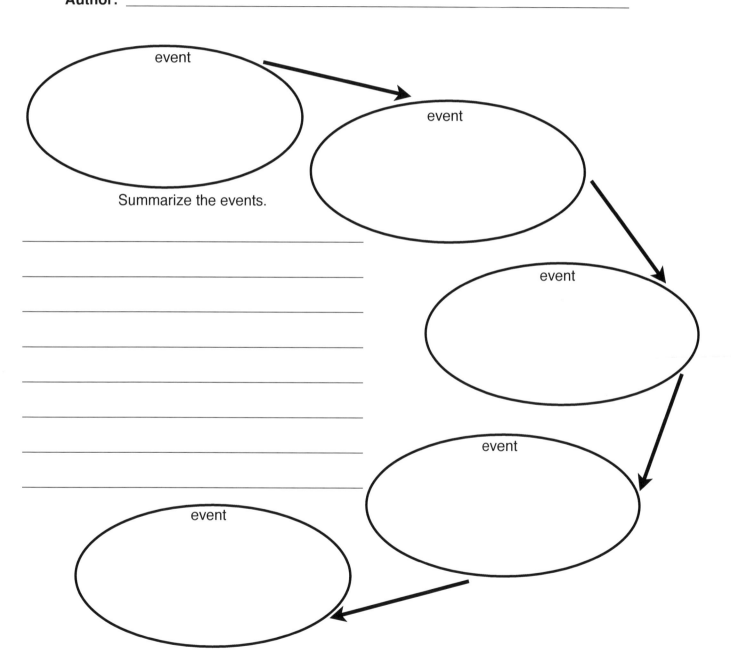

Summarize the events.

_____

_____

_____

_____

_____

_____

_____

Name: _____

Word Meaning

Directions: Read *Sir Cumference and the First Round Table*
by Cindy Neuschwander. Read the vocabulary words below that
"belong" to the story. Use picture information and clues to determine
the meanings of these words and phrases. Then, read the actual definition
in a resource book.

circumference
(Sir Cumference)

what I think it means

actual meaning I read in _____

geometry
(Geo of Metry)

what I think it means

actual meaning I read in _____

diameter
(Lady Di of Ameter)

what I think it means

actual meaning I read in _____

Can you come up with a new character that would live in this story?

_____

Name: _____

Word Meaning

Directions: Read *Germs Make Me Sick* by Melvin Berger. Read the vocabulary words below from the story. Use picture information and clues to determine the meanings of these words and phrases. Then, read the actual definition in a resource book.

virus

what I think it means

actual meaning I read in _____

germs

what I think it means

actual meaning I read in _____

bacteria

what I think it means

actual meaning I read in _____

antibodies

what I think it means

actual meaning I read in _____

Standard: Reading | Informational Text | RI.3.4   ©http://CoreCommonStandards.com

Name: _____

<u>Using the Text Features</u>

<u>Directions:</u> The text features below belong to a science article. Read the headings, captions, and keywords and look at the illustrations. Use the headings, captions, and keywords below to write a summary of what you think the article is about.

weight

Swept Away

Quick Rescue

massive

speed

People clear debris and dig out.

snow

force

Snow dogs smell victims and show rescuers where to dig.

_____

_____   _____

_____   _____

_____   _____

_____   _____

_____   _____

_____   _____

_____   _____

_____   _____

_____   _____

_____   _____

_____   _____

Standard: Reading I Informational Text I RI.3.5

Name: _____

Making a Resource Page

Directions: There are many text features found in informational texts. Find examples of the text features listed below. Write the resources you used to find these features. You can use things such as magazines, books, and web pages.

Text Feature	Resource	Example
ex: Heading	*National Geographic Kids* *Dec 2011/Jan 2012*	*Texting With Toes*
Heading		
Caption		
Table of Contents		
Index		
Glossary		
Reference		
Diagram		
Chart		
Cutaway View		
Photograph		
Graph		
Menu		
Hyperlink		
Bullet Points		

Standard: Reading I Informational Text I RI.3.5   ©http://CoreCommonStandards.com

Name: _____

Another View

Directions: Choose a biography to read. Select one that is told in third person, where the narrator is telling the story. Rewrite the story through the eyes of one of the other characters in the story. Be able to support your ideas with facts from the story. {*For example, read about Laura Ingalls Wilder and retell her life through her sister Mary's voice.*}

Story: _____

Author: _____

<u>Another View</u>

Directions: Choose a biography to read. Select one that is told in third person, where the narrator is telling the story. Rewrite the story through the eyes of one of the other characters in the story. Be able to support your ideas with facts from the story. {*For example, read about Laura Ingalls Wilder and retell her life through her sister Mary's voice.*}

In my version, I wrote _____

_____

_____

My reason for this is _____

_____

_____

In my version, I wrote _____

_____

_____

My reason for this is _____

_____

_____

In my version, I wrote _____

_____

_____

My reason for this is _____

_____

_____

Standard: Reading I Informational Text I RI.3.6   ©http://CoreCommonStandards.com

Name: _____

Finding Information

Directions: Read the following passage about *The Pony Express*. Use information gained from the illustration and the text to show your understanding of *The Pony Express*.

The Pony Express

The Pony Express delivered mail during the years 1860 and 1861 between St. Joseph, Missouri and Sacramento, California. This distance crossed the Great Plains, Rocky Mountains, and High Sierra. This service made it possible for mail to travel between the Atlantic and Pacific coasts in about 10 days.

Riders were young, aged between fifteen and twenty-five, rode horses at their top speed, stopping only to change horses, eat, or sleep.
Most days, riders covered 250 miles and people considered the riders to be very brave. But, after only 18 months, the service went bankrupt. The transcontinental telegraph took over.

Now, use the text and illustration to answer the questions.

[Advertisement illustration: "PONY EXPRESS! CHANGE OF TIME! REDUCED RATES! 10 Days to San Francisco! LETTERS WILL BE RECEIVED AT THE OFFICE, 84 BROADWAY, NEW YORK, Up to 4 P.M. every TUESDAY. AND Up to 2½ P.M. every SATURDAY, Which will be forwarded to connect with the PONY EXPRESS leaving ST. JOSEPH, Missouri, Every WEDNESDAY and SATURDAY at 11 P.M. TELEGRAMS Sent to Fort Kearney on the mornings of MONDAY and FRIDAY, to connect with PONY leaving St. Joseph, WEDNESDAYS and SATURDAYS. EXPRESS CHARGES. LETTERS weighing half ounce or under.......... $1 00 For every additional half ounce or fraction of an ounce 1 00 In all cases to be enclosed in 10 cent Government Stamped Envelopes, And all Express CHARGES Pre-paid. PONY EXPRESS ENVELOPES For Sale at our Office. WELLS, FARGO & CO., Ag'ts. New York, July 1, 1861."]

1. Between what states did the Pony Express travel? _____

2. How long did the Pony Express service last? _____

3. How much did a letter under a half-ounce cost? _____

4. Why did the Pony Express stop delivering mail? _____

5. Between what ages were most Pony Express riders? _____

6. About how many days would a letter take to get from one coast of the country to the other? _____

7. Once the Pony Express ended, how did people get their mail? _____

Standard: Reading I Informational Text I RI.3.7   ©http://CoreCommonStandards.com

Name: _____

Using the Text and Illustrations

Directions: Read a chosen selection of informational text. Use information gained from the illustrations and the text to show your understanding of what you read. Write and answer several *what, where, when, how,* and *why* questions about the text.

Story: _____

Author: _____

Topic: _____

Write questions and answers about the text and illustration.	Describe or draw a picture or diagram from the text and how it helped you gain information about the text.

Name: _____

The Beginning of the Revolutionary War

Directions: Read the sentences below about how the Revolutionary War began. Cut the strips and paste them in order onto page 2. Explain why you chose this particular order of events.

Explain why you chose this order of events:

_____

_____

_____

_____

_____

_____

_____

_____

_____

In 1773, after the Tea Tax was issued by the British government, the Sons of Liberty, a militant group, boarded the vessel carrying the British tea and threw the tea into the harbor.   This prompted the British to issue, what the colonists called, The Intolerable Acts, which authorized officials to strictly control the colonies.

The British crown issued many taxes onto the colonists, such as the Stamp Tax, and taxes on paint, paper, and glass.

The colonists formed the Continental Congress. Soon after, the Revolutionary war began.

The Boston Massacre, a battle between British soldiers and Boston townspeople, occurred in 1770.

The colonists boycotted British goods and many of the taxes were repealed, but there was much resentment towards the British.

Standard: Reading I Informational Text I RI.3.8   ©http://CoreCommonStandards.com

Name: _____

The Beginning of the Revolutionary War

Cut the strips and paste them in order. Explain, on page 1, why you chose this order of events.

Name: _____

Making Connections

Directions: Read an informational story about a scientific discovery or historical event. Look for the events in the story which illustrate cause and effect situations. Write the causes in one column and their effects in the other.

Story: _____

Author: _____

Topic: _____

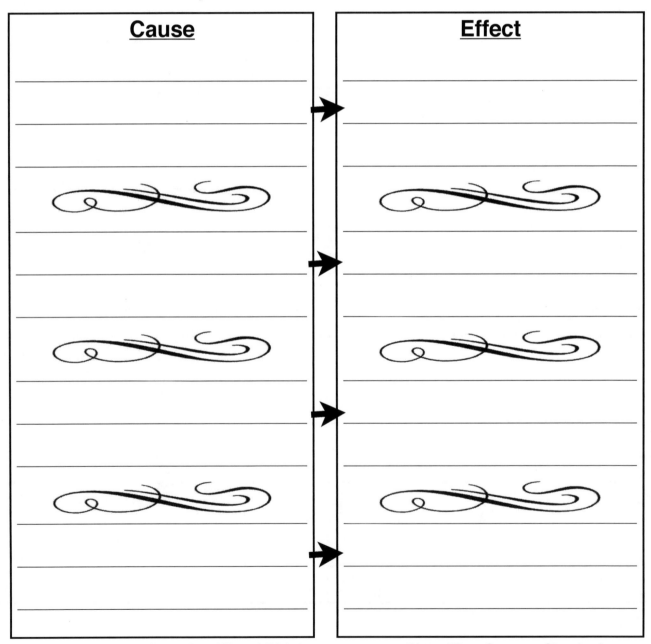

Cause	**Effect**

Name: _____

Compare & Contrast

Directions: After reading two different texts about the same event or topic, compare and contrast the key details of both.

Event or Topic_____

Text: _____ Author: _____	Text: _____ Author: _____

Similarities

Differences

Differences

©http://CoreCommonStandards.com

Name: _____

Level: Third Grade

Compare & Contrast

Directions: After reading two different texts about the same event or topic, compare and contrast the key details of both.

Event or Topic _____

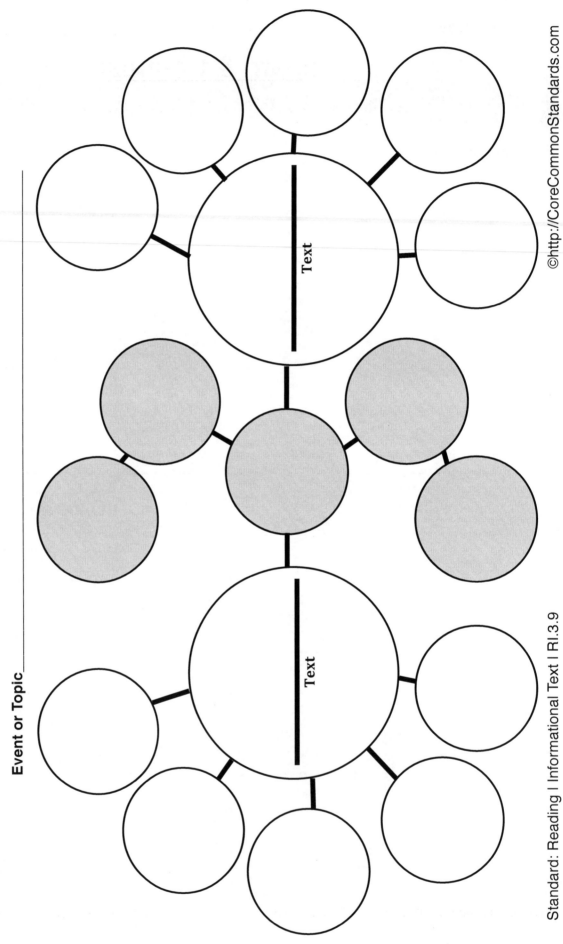

Standard: Reading I Informational Text I RI.3.9

Name: _____

Nonfiction I Am Reading

Directions: Keep track of the nonfiction text you read this year in Third Grade. When you finish a book, write the title and the date you completed the book. What was the topic?

Date	Book Title	Topic

Standard: Reading I Informational Text I RI.3.10   ©http://CoreCommonStandards.com

Level: Third Grade   Name: _____

What Are They Reading?

Directions: Keep track of the nonfiction text your students can read this year at grade
Write the date each type of text was read successfully.

Name	nonfiction storybook	photo-graphic essay	auto-biography	informational book	journal/ diary

Standard: Reading I Informational Text I RI.3.10   ©http://CoreCommonStandards.com

Name: _____

Prefixes and Suffixes

Directions: Read the words below. Take note of the prefixes and derivational suffixes. Write the root word for each and what each prefix and suffix means.

Word	Root Word	suffix/prefix meaning
emigration		
unnecessary		
sincerely		
disappear		
predetermine		
exclamation		
spoonful		
tourist		
government		
rebuild		
gymnastic		

Standard: Reading I Foundational Skills I RF.3.3   ©http://CoreCommonStandards.com

Name: _____

Just Irregular

Directions: Some words are spelled irregularly. That means their spellings do not follow common patterns. Read the words below. Write how you think the word might be spelled if it followed regular spelling patterns.

Irregularly Spelled Word	The Way The Spelling Sounds
friend	frend
many	
come	
said	
enough	
could	
chaos	
ocean	
bologna	
climb	

Standard: Reading l Foundational Skills l RF.3.3

©http://CoreCommonStandards.com

Reading With Fluency
nonfiction

Directions: When you read, you are not just saying the words. Readers read with a purpose and to understand. Practice reading orally so that you can be a fluent reader.

Read the passage below while your teacher times you. Try to read as many words accurately as you can in one minute. Try again in a couple of weeks to see if your fluency improves. {Goal of 130 WPM}

The Bottlenose Dolphin

The bottlenose dolphin is one of the most intelligent marine mammals. Many people think that the dolphin is a fish, but they are actually mammals. In order for an animal to be a "mammal", it must be warm- blooded, have hair on its skin, and the female must produce milk for its young.

The bottlenose dolphin gets its name from its bottle-shaped snout. Their curved mouths give them the appearance that they are smiling. Bottlenose dolphins usually weigh between 400 and 600 pounds and grow to be about 10 feet long. The lifespan of a dolphin can be 30 to 50 years of age. The bottlenose dolphin likes to eat bottom-dwelling fish, octopus, and squid.

This animal likes to have fun just like we do! Bottlenose dolphins love to play in the warm tropical waters and usually stay with a group of other dolphins. If these dolphins need to defend themselves from their predator, they will give off a high-pitched sound, called echolocation; "Click, Click, Click!"

Date	Words Read Correctly Per Minute

Standard: Reading I Foundational Skills I RF.3.4　　　　©http://CoreCommonStandards.com

Name: _____

Reading With Fluency

fiction

Directions: When you read, you are not just saying the words. Readers read with a purpose and to understand. Practice reading orally so that you can be a fluent reader.

Read the passage below while your teacher times you. Try to read as many words accurately as you can in one minute. Try again in a couple of weeks to see if your fluency improves. {Goal of 130 WPM}

The Lonely Goldfish

Sam has a goldfish. He keeps his goldfish in a small bowl next to his bed. Sam is careful not to over feed his goldfish and makes sure he has clean water and is happy. One day Sam said to his Mom, "I don't think Tinker is very happy." "Why do you say that?" asked Mom. Sam told his Mom that Tinker has no one to swim with and that he sometimes just sits behind his toy tree in his bowl. "Do you think Tinker would be happy to have another fish to swim with him?" asked his Mom. "Yes!" cried Sam. "That would be great!"

The next day, after Sam came home from school, he and his Mom went to the pet store to buy another goldfish friend for Tinker. The store had only three goldfish left. Sam could not decide which one he wanted to take home. He thought and thought but could not pick a friend for Tinker. Finally, Mom said to the man at the pet store, "We'll take all three." "Wow!" yelled Sam. "That would be great!" "Tinker will not be lonely anymore."

Because Sam and his Mom bought three fish, they had to buy a bigger bowl so the fish would have plenty of room to swim, and they even bought another toy for the new family of fish. When Sam got home and put all the fish together in their new bowl, Tinker started swimming so fast. Sam knew Tinker was now a happy fish and no longer lonely. He spent the night thinking of three names for his new fish and watched them all get along while he sat on his bed. Sam was not lonely either!

Date	Words Read Correctly Per Minute

Standard: Reading I Foundational Skills I RF.3.4   ©http://CoreCommonStandards.com

Name: _____

Supporting an Opinion

Directions: Write an opinion piece about a current news or school issue that is important to you. Provide reasons and explain how these reasons support your opinion. Write a concluding statement. Share your opinion with a partner.

Topic: _____

My
Opinion

My
Reasons

How my reasons support my opinion: _____

_____

_____

_____

Concluding Statement: _____

_____

_____

_____

Standard: Reading | Writing | W.3.1   ©http://CoreCommonStandards.com

Level: Third Grade   Name: _____

Supporting an Opinion

Directions: Write an opinion piece about a current news or school issue that is important to you. Provide reasons and explain how these reasons support your opinion. Write a concluding statement. Share your opinion with a partner.

Topic: _____

My Opinion: _____

_____

_____

Reason #1:

_____

_____

_____

_____

Reason #2:

_____

_____

_____

_____

Reason #3:

_____

_____

_____

_____

Reason #4:

_____

_____

_____

_____

Standard: Reading I Writing I W.3.1   ©http://CoreCommonStandards.com

Name: _____

To Inform and Explain

Directions: Explain in writing how to stay healthy. Develop the topic with facts, definitions, and details. Use illustrations if needed and provide a concluding statement.

Title: _____

Vocabulary Words and Definitions About Staying Healthy

Details and Facts About Staying Healthy

Illustration

Illustration

My concluding statement: _____

_____

_____

Name: _____

To Inform and Explain

Directions: Choose a topic about which to write that informs or explains. Write what you know about the topic, and what you learned after researching. Choose the information you think would best explain your topic. Write a beginning paragraph below.

My possible topics: (Circle selected topic)

1. _____   2. _____

3. _____   4. _____

What I Know	**What I Have Learned**

Highlight or circle the facts you think are most important for your topic.

Write a beginning paragraph...

_____

_____

_____

_____

_____

_____

Standard: Reading I Writing I W.3.2   ©http://CoreCommonStandards.com

Real Life Narrative

Directions: Think about an experience you have had in your life. It may be a positive experience, or perhaps, a negative one. Include a main idea based on you, and a sequence of events from your life at the time of the experience. Include a strong closing statement. Use the organizer below to prepare your narrative.

Title

_____

Experience

_____

Main Idea

_____

_____

Event	Event	Event
_____ _____ _____	_____ _____ _____	_____ _____ _____
Event	Event	Event
_____ _____ _____	_____ _____ _____	_____ _____ _____

Closing Statement

_____

_____

_____

Fictional Narrative

Directions: Create an experience you have wanted to have in your life. Include a main idea based on you, and a sequence of events that would occur at the time of the experience. Include a strong closing statement. Use the organizer below to prepare your narrative.

Title

_____

Experience

_____

Main Idea

_____

_____

Event	Event	Event
_____ _____ _____	_____ _____ _____	_____ _____ _____

Event	Event	Event
_____ _____ _____	_____ _____ _____	_____ _____ _____

Closing Statement

_____

_____

_____

_____

Standard: Reading I Writing I W.3.3   ©http://CoreCommonStandards.com

Name: _____

Writing in Third Grade

Directions: Produce writing that demonstrates the development and organization expected in third grade.

Write opinion pieces

☐ Introduce the topic

☐ State an opinion

☐ Create an organized structure that lists reasons

☐ Provide a concluding statement

Write informative/explanatory text

☐ Introduce the topic

☐ Group related information together

☐ Include illustrations when useful

☐ Develop the topic with facts, definitions, and details

☐ Connect ideas with linking words (also, another, and, more, but)

Write narratives of real or imaginary events

☐ Use descriptive details

☐ Use clear sequence

☐ Use dialogue and descriptions of actions, thoughts, and feelings

☐ Use temporal words and phrases (time order)

☐ Provide a sense of closure

Standard: Reading | Writing | W.3.4   ©http://CoreCommonStandards.com

Writing in Third Grade

Directions: Choose a format, pick a topic, and write. Be aware of the expectations in third grade writing.

Opinion Piece

My topic:

My position:

Informative/Explanatory Piece

My topic:

My purpose:

Narrative Piece

My topic:

My audience:

Name: _____

Editors

Directions: After completing a piece of writing, use this chart to edit your writing for spelling and other conventions. Work with a partner...maybe they will see something you missed. Fix your errors. Think about why they needed to be corrected.

Mark	Description	Example
∧	insert	is What time dinner? ∧ Is this for the tree or for the flowers? ,∧
≡	capitalize	Sanchez lives in poland. ≡
⧣	add space	⧣ Betty dancedwith her troupe. ∧
↗	delete	She went with ~~with~~ him to the beach.
⌒	close space	The beetle ate ⌒ the aphid.
¶	new paragraph	So they sat on the porch and watched the parade. ¶ The next week, Danny and Paul went for a long trip on their canoe.
⑤℗	spelling error	⑤℗ Papa likes to golg in the morning.
∼	transpose	Diane and ~~friend her~~ sewed a blanket.
⊙	add period	Mom likes her coffee in the morning⊙ She puts coffee in for her.

Standard: Reading I Writing I W.3.5

Level: Third Grade   Name: _____

Revising

Directions: After completing a piece of writing, use this chart to revise your writing. Work with a partner...maybe they will see something you missed. Improve your writing. Listen to how it sounds.

☐   1. Does the beginning grab (or hook) the reader's attention?

☐   2. Are all of the possible questions answered?
         Did I answer Who? What? Where? When? Why? How?

☐   3. Are my words interesting? Should I change one for another?

☐   4. Is there enough detail to express feelings and thoughts?

☐   5. Do I need to add more details, reasons, or examples?

☐   6. Have I used enough descriptive words so the reader can picture what I am writing about?

☐   7. Do I use varied sentence beginnings?

☐   8. Did I use figurative language such as similes, metaphors, vivid verbs, onomatopoeia, and adjectives?

☐   9. Do my sentences stay focused on the topic?

☐   10. Does the writing flow sequentially?

☐   11. Does the ending bring the piece to a close?

Standard: Reading I Writing I W.3.5   ©http://CoreCommonStandards.com

Name: _____

Using Technology

Directions: Write a story. Use the computer to create and present your writing.

My topic is...

_____

I am going to use a computer to create my story.

I want to add pictures to my story by using...

a. *digital camera*   b. *scanner*   c. *clipart*

I will share my writing by...

a. *printing my story*
b. *emailing it to my classmates*
c. *presenting it using a projector*
d. *creating a powerpoint presentation*
e. *using a movie-making program*

computer tools

spell check
font
word art

online tools

thesaurus
dictionary
clipart
animation

writing checklist

prewriting	
drafting	
revising	
word choice	
sentence structure	
editing	
punctuation	
capitalization	
spelling	

What I need to add/change/delete...

_____

_____

_____

_____

_____

_____

_____

_____

Standard: Reading l Writing l W.3.6

©http://CoreCommonStandards.com

Name: _____

Using Digital Resources

Directions: Today, many people use digital tools to write. Use this checklist to record what digital skills each student can perform.

Digital Skill	Date	Success
Uses a mouse well. (Can double-click; move cursor to desired place; scroll if available.)		
Knows where all common characters are on keyboard.		
Knows how to use space bar; back space; delete; and return.		
Can log in and out of programs.		
Can change the font or size of font.		
Can add a graphic.		
Can drag and drop an item.		
Can copy/paste an item.		
Can save a file.		
Can print work.		
Can create a Powerpoint Presentation.		
Can locate information on the internet.		
Can send an email.		
Can attach a file to an email.		

Standard: Reading I Writing I W.3.6

Name: _____

Research Projects

Directions: Choose a topic to research. Use various research tools to learn about your topic and obtain information to present to others. Record information in the organizer below.

My Topic: _____

Resources I used: _____

_____

_____

information	**information**

information	**information**

Research Projects

Directions: Choose a topic to research. Use various research tools to learn about your topic and obtain information to present to others. Include a bibliography to cite your resources. Use this sheet to help you write your bibliography.

For a Book:

Author Name: _____,_____
                      (last name)   (first name)   (second name or initial)

Second Author: _____,_____
                      (last name)   (first name)   (second name or initial)

Title Underlined: _____

Location Book was Published: _____

Publisher Name: _____

Copyright Date: _____

Example: Cox, Clinton. <u>Mark Twain America's Humorist, Dreamer, Prophet: a Biography.</u>
          New York Scholastic, 1995.

For the Internet:

Author Name: _____,_____
                      (last name)   (first name)   (second name or initial)
Second Author: _____,_____
                      (last name)   (first name)   (second name or initial)

Web article title in quotes: _____

Website Title Underlined: _____

Date website was accessed by you_____

Website url: _____

Example: Blount, Roy. "Mark Twain: Our Original Superstar." <u>Time Magazine U.S.</u> 2008.
          Time Magazine Online. 3 July, 2008.
              http://www.time.com/time/magazine/article/0,9171,1820166,00.html

Level: Third Grade   Name: _____

Taking Notes
Real vs Fantasy

Directions: While listening to a story or watching a movie or video, take notes about what is reality in the story, and what is fantasy.

Title: _____

Author or Director: _____

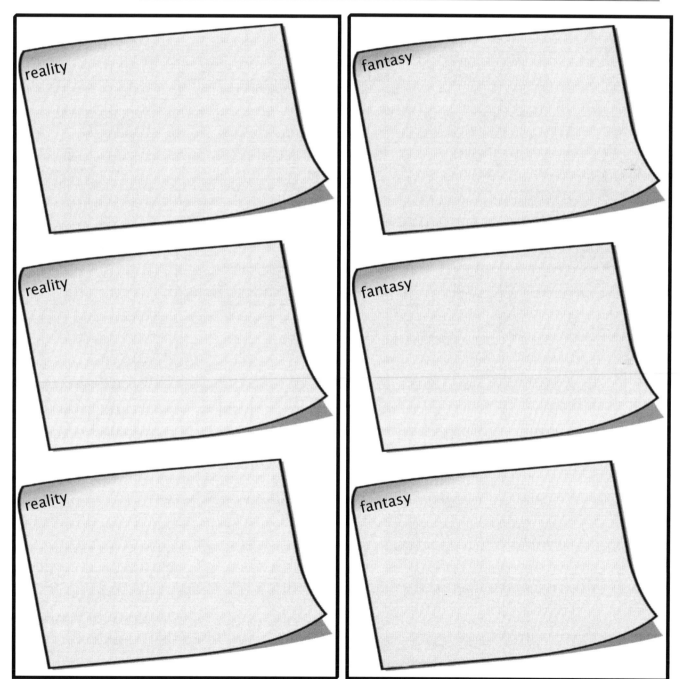

Level: Third Grade   Name: _____

Taking Notes

Directions: Use this organizer to take notes on a topic you are studying. Write a summary.

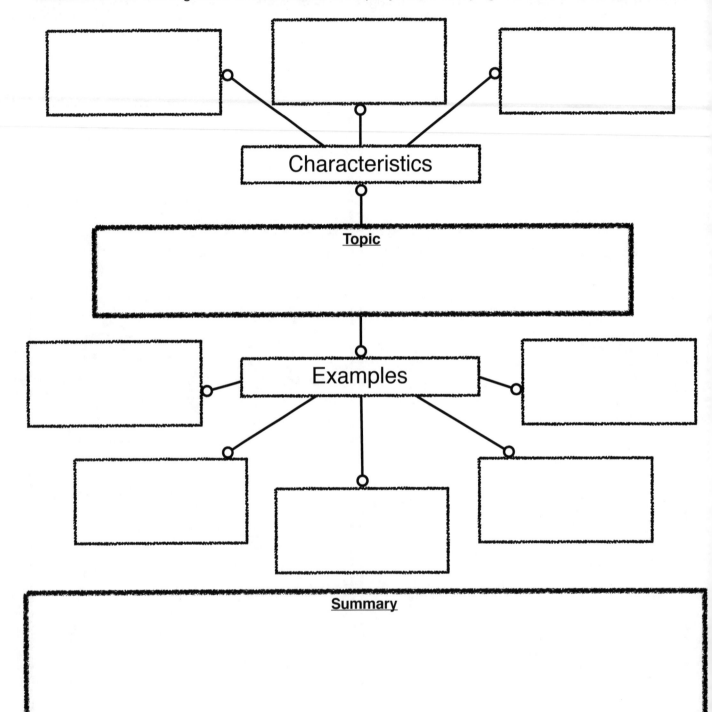

Name: _____

Writing in Different Genres

Directions: Use this chart to record the types of writing you do, the dates, the audience, and the purpose for the writing.

Writing Genre	Date	Audience	Purpose
Journal Entry			
Scientific Research Paper			
Historical Research paper			
Biography			
Autobiography			
Poem			
Song			
Adventure Story			
Realistic Fiction			
Nonfiction Story			
Informational Writing			
Procedural Writing			
Interview			
News Story			
Letter			

Standard: Reading I Writing I W.3.10   ©http://CoreCommonStandards.com

Name: _____

Daily Writing

Directions: *When writers write, we sometimes spend several days, or even weeks, working on a particular piece. Sometimes, a piece of writing may be completed in only a few hours, or minutes. Writers write for many reasons. But no matter what is written, the writer should think about the purpose of the piece, and the audience...or who will be reading it.*

Use this chart to keep track of writing you complete. Try to vary the genres in which you write. Keep in mind the purpose and audience for each piece.

Title of Piece/Genre	Date	Audience	Purpose

Standard: Reading I Writing I W.3.10

Name: _____

Small Group Discussions

Directions: When we meet for discussions in Third Grade, we contribute to the group by following agreed-upon rules. Use this form during discussions to keep track of how well you participate.

☐ I Wait my Turn and Gain the Floor respectfully

☐ I Listen To Others with Care

☐ I Stay on Topic

☐ I Respect Others' Ideas

☐ I Ask Questions

☐ I Offer Constructive Criticism

Something I learned during today's discussion about _____ was

_____

_____

_____

_____

Name: _____

Taking Notes

Directions: Watch a video about a topic you are studying in class. Think about the information presented and write the main idea of the video. Add supporting details. Write a summative sentence about the video.

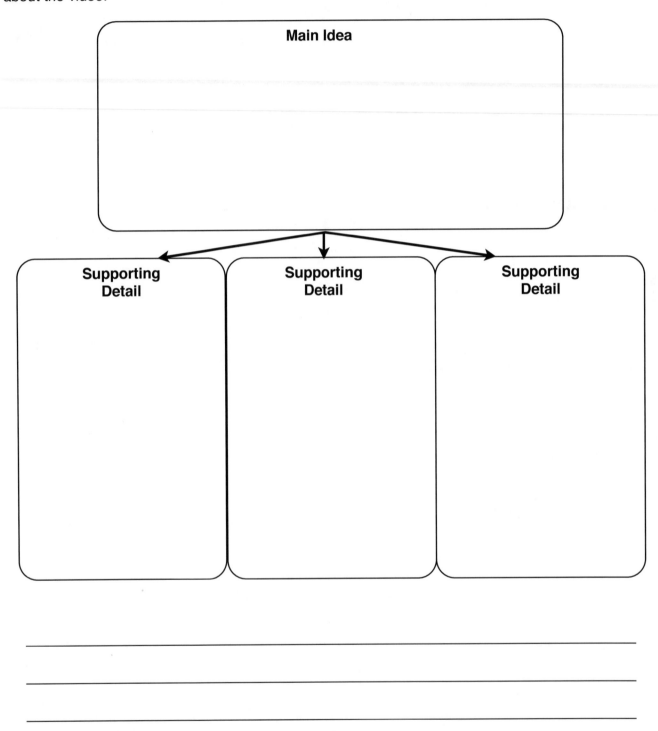

_____

_____

_____

Standard: Reading I Speaking & Listening I SL.3.2   ©http://CoreCommonStandards.com

Level: Third Grade   Name: _____

Asking Questions

Directions: Listen to a guest speaker who is visiting your school or class, or watch a speaker online discuss a particular topic.   Ask open and closed questions to gain information. Record any answers in your own words.

Questioning takes practice. Asking the right question is important in gathering the information needed.

Types of questions:
Closed Question: A closed question usually receives a short, factual answer. For example, "Are you hot?" The answer could be "Yes," or "No." Or, "Where is the Church?" An address may be the answer.

Open Questions: Open questions usually receive longer, more detailed answers. These questions usually begin with *why, what*, or *how*. The open questions asks the respondent for his or her knowledge, opinions, or feelings. Asking for someone to describe some idea or topic is also way of asking an open question.

Question: (Closed or Open-Ended)

_____

_____

Answer:

_____

_____

_____

Question: (Closed or Open-Ended)

_____

_____

Answer:

_____

_____

_____

Question: (Closed or Open-Ended)

_____

_____

Answer:

_____

_____

_____

Standard: Reading I Speaking & Listening I SL.3.3   ©http://CoreCommonStandards.com

Name: _____

Report on a Topic

Write a newspaper article on a hot topic. Recount with appropriate facts and relevant, descriptive details. Share your article, speaking clearly at an understandable pace.

Name of article: _____

Who: _____

_____

What: _____

_____

_____

_____

When: _____

_____

Where: _____

_____

picture:

caption:

How: _____

_____

Why: _____

_____

Summary: _____

_____

_____

_____

_____

_____

_____

Level: Third Grade   Name: _____

Make an Audio Recording

Directions: Create an audio recording of a poem or story. It can be a story from your classroom collection, the library, or one you or a classmate has written. Use a computer, iPod, iPad, or digital recorder to record your voice. Use fluid reading and speak with interest in order to express, emphasize, or enhance certain facts or details. Don't forget to include your own point of view.

There are several programs available for children to use to create digital stories. Some are listed below.

For Microsoft Products
Photostory ...free program using still photos or graphics and added audio

Powerpoint

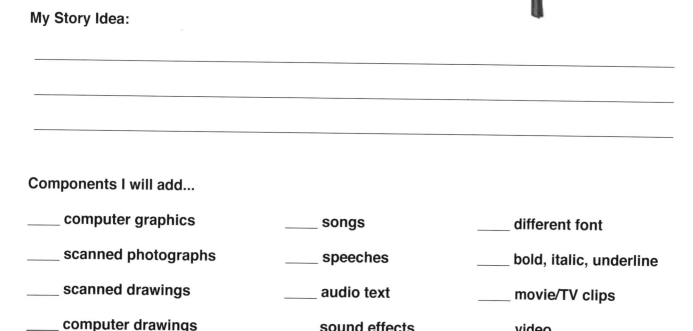

For Apple Products
My Story-Book Maker ...App for iPad/iPod/iPhone ($)
    make drawings and record your voice

Writer's Studio ...App for iPad/iPod/iPhone ($)
    make drawings, add photos, and record your voice

iMovie ...usually included in Mac purchase

Keynote (like Powerpoint) included in iWorks

My Story Idea:

_____

_____

_____

Components I will add...

_____ **computer graphics**	_____ **songs**	_____ **different font**
_____ **scanned photographs**	_____ **speeches**	_____ **bold, italic, underline**
_____ **scanned drawings**	_____ **audio text**	_____ **movie/TV clips**
_____ **computer drawings**	_____ **sound effects**	_____ **video**

Standard: Reading I Speaking & Listening I SL.3.5   ©http://CoreCommonStandards.com

Name: _____

Speaking in Complete Sentences

Directions: Write sentences that explain, in detail, about something you are studying in Science. Use complete, descriptive sentences, that provide clarification and explanation. Share your writing with the class using a clear voice while speaking in complete sentences.

Use vocabulary associated with your topic to enhance your writing.

Standard: Reading I Speaking & Listening I SL.3.6

©http://CoreCommonStandards.com

Name: _____

Adverbs Adverbs

Directions: Complete the sentences with the adverbs listed below. Explain the function of the adverb for each sentence. Ex: *He ate quickly during his break.* **Quickly** *describes how fast he ate.*

finally   **patiently**   **brightly**   **shyly**   **quietly**   **loudly**

Sample: He ate **quickly** during his break.

Explain: Quickly describes how fast he ate. _____

1. We played _____ when the lights went out.

Explain: _____

2. The flame burned _____ on the candle.

Explain: _____

3. Mom _____ waited while I got my shoes on.

Explain: _____

4. The mama bird chirped _____ as the cat walked by.

Explain: _____

5. My sister _____ hid behind my dad's leg.

Explain: _____

6. Natasha _____ gave the teachers their new books.

Explain: _____

Name: _____

Agreement

Directions: Complete the sentences with the appropriate form of the verb and circle the one that best fits the sentence. Be sure the subject of the sentence agrees with the verb's form.

1. Spike _____ his dog food in a porcelain bowl.

Which verb best fits in the sentence above?   **eat**   **eats**

2. Claus and his brother, Hans, _____ on the Polar Express.

Which verb best fits in the sentence above?   **ride**   **rides**

3. Pierre _____ to play Boggle with his mémé.

Which verb best fits in the sentence above?   **like**   **likes**

4. The three cardinals _____ for their mom to fly back with worms.

Which verb best fits in the sentence above?   **wait**   **waits**

5. The Scoop Shack _____ 3-scoop sundaes for $2.00.

Which verb best fits in the sentence above?   **sell**   **sells**

6. Chef DelRosario _____ wonderful Spanish cuisine.

Which verb best fits in the sentence above?   **cook**   **cooks**

7. The rocks in the garden _____ when the dog plays there.

Which verb best fits in the sentence above?   **roll**   **rolls**

8. Captain Hall and Officer Collins _____ to the man in the street.

Which verb best fits in the sentence above?   **talk**   **talks**

Comparative and Superlative Adjectives

Directions: Complete the sentences with the appropriate form of the adjective. Change or add to the given adjective to make it correct.

1. The pillar with the flag is the _____ pillar on the field.

far

2. Anthony ate _____ cookies than his brother.

few

3. Stan has pledged to eat _____ from now on.

healthy

4. The bulb on the lamp seems _____ than the one on the wall.

bright

5. At school, we saw the _____ puppet show!

amazing

6. Saturday's meeting was _____ than last week's.

fun

7. I will cross the river farther down because it is _____ than here.

shallow

8. Paula has a _____ laptop than I do.

new

Name: _____

Fixing Sentences

Directions: Read the sentences below. Correct the words that need capital letters, insert quotation marks { " " } and apostrophes {'} and add the correct punctuation at the end. { . ! ? }

1	candace and margaret went to the uso dance last night
2	the korean war lasted from june 25 1950 to july 27 1953
3	june 6 1944 is also known as d day
4	sergeant roy joined his outfit in livingston louisiana in 1863
5	the first shots rang out on april 19 1775 in lexington ma
6	the lusitania sunk in 1915 bringing the us into world war 1
7	president roosevelt said december 7 1941 a date which will live in infamy
8	operation desert shield began on august 7 1990 when troops were sent to saudi arabia
9	robert ran to sonnys grocery with a ration coupon to buy some sugar
10	why was the united states changed forever on september 11 2001
11	the american red cross was founded by clara barton in the late 1800s
12	the united states entered the vietnam war to fight communism

Standard: Reading I Language I L.3.2

©http://CoreCommonStandards.com

Name: _____

Fixing Spelling

Directions: Read the text below. Correct the words that are misspelled. Circle the misspelled words and write the correct spelling above each word.

Harriet Tubman is well nown for risking her life as a "conductor" in the Underground Railroad, which led eskaped slaves to freedim in the north. But did you know that the forma slave also served as a spie for the Union during the Sivil War and was the first women in American historey to lead a military expedition?

During a time when women were ushuly restricted to tradishunal roles like cooking and nurseing, she did her share of those jobs. But she allso worked side-by-side with men, says riter Tom Allen, who tells her exciting story in the National Geographic book, Harriet Tubman, Secret Ajent.

Tubman decided to help the Union Army becuase she wanted freedom for all of the people who were forced into slavrey, not just the few she could help by herself. And she convinsed many other brave African Americans to join her as spies, even at the risk of being hanged if they were cawght.

Name: _____

Plural vs Possessive

Directions: Complete the sentences with the appropriate plural or possessive word.

1. Mom gave _____ bowl to my sister so she could fill it.

Kittys   Kitty's

2. Bobby bought fifteen _____ to give to his friends.

lollipops   lollipop's

3. The _____ leaves are beginning to change color.

trees   tree's

4. We watched a play performed by _____ class.

Mrs. Clarks   Mrs. Clark's

5. All of the _____ on the floor belong to Leif.

toys   toy's

6. Last night, the _____ in the sky shimmered.

stars   star's

Choose the correct plural, possessive, or plural-possessive form of the word below.

7. *I drew a picture with _____ for my _____ birthday.

crayons crayon's crayons'   moms mom's moms'

8. *In my _____ tree there is a huge _____ nest.

aunts aunt's aunts'   bees bee's bees'

Standard: Reading I Language I L.3.2   ©http://CoreCommonStandards.com

Name: _____

Spoken vs Written

Directions: Rodney and Hank are discussing their new invention; the Automatic Dog-Walker 2000. They will be sending the prototype to a business called Invention Central. Write dialogue between the two characters. Use informal conversation with appropriate words and punctuation for the dialogue.

Now, create the letter they wrote to the company. Use formal writing with proper words and punctuation.

Name: _____

Writing with Effect

Directions: Write a sentence to describe each of the pictures below. Use descriptive words and phrases such as adjectives, adverbs, idioms, metaphors, and similes for effect.

Name: _____

Spoken or Written?

Directions: Read the texts below. Thinking about the word choice and conventions used, write whether the text is formal spoken, formal written, informal spoken, or informal written.

"My mom said I chill at your crib next week. That's so awesome!"

_____

Thank you, Mr. Thomas, for visiting our class last week and speaking to us about butterflies and their importance.
                    Sincerely, John

_____

One day, he decided to leave his home in Hannibal, Missouri, and set out west to find his fortune in gold.

_____

OMG!!! Ur not seeeerius!! Have to chow now. L8R!

_____

"Hello. I would like to speak to someone about opening a new savings account."

_____

Dad, I am at Sarah's. Mom left chop suey in the fridge. Be home later. Love ya.
                    -Kate

_____

"Hey dude, you wanna go catch a flick tonight?"

_____

"Thank you for calling McPatty's Irish Cafe. How may I help you?"

_____

Standard: Reading I Language I L.3.3

Name: _____

Multiple Meanings

Directions: Match the multiple meaning words below to the pictures that define their meanings. Each word has two matches.

duck

ring

skate

slide

bowl

court

Name: _____

Making New Words

Directions: Read the word on the left. Add the affix (prefix or suffix) provided. Write the meaning of the new word.

ex: patriot   -ism   patriotism   devotion to one's country

word	affix	new word	meaning
manage	-able	_____	
puzzle	-ment	_____	
cycle	uni-	_____	
advise	-or	_____	
biography	auto-	_____	
wish	-ful	_____	
brother	-hood	_____	
focal	bi-	_____	
colored	multi-	_____	

Standard: Reading l Language l L.3.4

Name: _____

Defining Words

Directions: Using a dictionary, print or digital, locate key words and write the meanings. Use this form to write key vocabulary words and phrases associated with a topic you are studying in class.

Resources used:

Print: _____

_____

Digital: _____

_____

word	definition

Standard: Reading I Language I L.3.4   ©http://CoreCommonStandards.com

Name: _____

Figurative Language

Directions: Read the examples of nonliteral, figurative language below. Write what type each example is. Use the definitions of each type to help you.

hyperbole (exaggerating for emphasis or effect)
metaphor (a comparison between two like things, but not using the words "as" and "like")
personification (where an object or idea is given human characteristics)
simile (a comparison between two like things using the words "as" and "like")
idiom (very common usage of certain metaphors, similes, hyperbole, and personification)

The brown grass was begging for water. _____	The burden is my cross to bear. _____	She's making a mountain out of a molehill. _____
Last winter was as long as a sad story. _____	He was 40 feet tall! _____	I am so tired I could sleep for a year. _____
This shirt is a thousand years old. _____	He bit off more than he could chew. _____	The crowd was buzzing like a beehive. _____
That guy is barking up the wrong tree. _____	I am doing a million things at once! _____	She planted the seeds of wisdom in her. _____
He hung his head like a wilted flower. _____	The angry storm pounded the camper's roof. _____	They popped out of their seats like toast from a toaster. _____
Aw, I am just pulling your leg. _____	We must wait for the wheels of justice to turn. _____	The greedy weeds have starved my daffodils. _____

Standard: Reading | Language | L.3.5

Name: _____

Figurative Language

Directions: Complete the graphic organizer with a key word from a subject you are studying. Think about the relationship of the key word to the information you write in the boxes below. Write a sentence that provides an example of the key word's meaning.

Synonyms	Antonyms

Key Word

Illustrations	Definition

_____

_____

_____

Name: _____

Certain About That?

Directions: Distinguish the range of meaning among the related words below that describe degrees of certainty. Rank each word with a degree of certainty: *weak* or *strong*
Then, write a sentence for each word.

Word	Degree of Certainty	Sentence
Sample know	**strong**	I <u>know</u> that someone is in the room.
certain	_____	
unlikely	_____	
undoubtedly	_____	
perhaps	_____	
definitely	_____	
possibly	_____	
wonder	_____	
might	_____	
probably	_____	

Standard: Reading l Language l L.3.5

©http://CoreCommonStandards.com

Level: Third Grade

Name: _____

Word Study

Directions: Use this semantic map to better understand a key word from your studies. Create symbols, draw pictures, and write words (synonyms) that illustrate the meaning of the word.

Topic of Study: _____

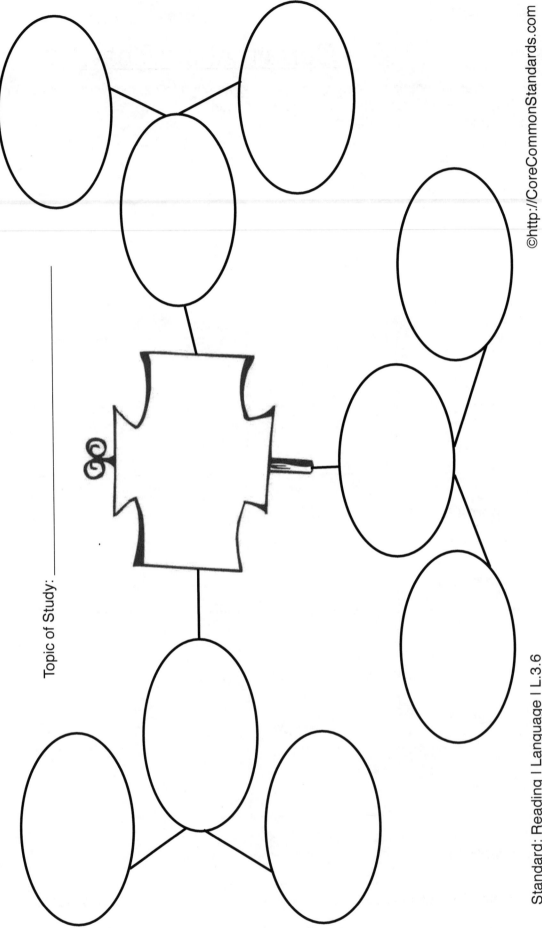

Standard: Reading I Language I L.3.6

Name: _____

Spatial Words

Directions: Fill in the blank with the correct spatial word.

1. The marbles fell out of the bag and rolled _____ the couch.

between   **beneath**   **aboard**

2. My sister and I walked _____ the street to the candy store.

away   **amongst**   **across**

3. Paul was sitting _____ his bike while he waited for Tim to show.

astride   **amid**   **around**

4. The elephants walked _____ the big top tent.

below   **ahead**   **toward**

5. Morgan and Riley both teach _____ the new school building.

onto   **within**   **apart**

6. Last night, the Jones family went _____ a cruise ship.

between   **near**   **aboard**

7. My grandpa likes to hide his money _____ the mattress.

underneath   **round**   **outside**

8. Our new shed that dad built is just _____ the chicken coop.

down   **beyond**   **up**

Standard: Reading | Language | L.3.6

Name: _____

Temporal Words

Directions: Fill in the blank with the correct temporal word or phrase.

1. I did my homework and will hand it in _____.

once again   **tomorrow**   **last night**

2. Sandy will go on stage _____ Timothy and his Blue Band.

prior to   **yesterday**   **formerly**

3. I am in third grade and _____ I will be in fourth grade.

previously   **last night**   **next year**

4. She let go of the handlebars and _____ fell off her bike.

however   **meanwhile**   **subsequently**

5. The movie and the basketball game were on TV _____.

finally   **concurrently**   **prior to**

6. First, we will have cake, _____ opening the presents.

immediately   **followed by**   **after**

7. _____, we need to write a draft; then we can finalize it.

previously   **before**   **first of all**

8. The storm destroyed the chairs, so _____ they brought them inside.

thereafter   **next**   **yearly**

Standard: Reading I Language I L.3.6

©http://CoreCommonStandards.com

Common Core State Standards

Third Grade Worksheets Common Core Workbook

Grade 3

•Math Standards

Worksheets that teach every Common Core Standard!

Name: _____

Show the Product

Directions: For the multiplication equations below, create an array, show multiple addition, or write a number story to illustrate the product.

3 X 5	3 X 5	3 X 5
This array shows 15.	3 + 3 + 3 + 3 + 3 = 15	I had three bags. Each bag had 5 marbles inside. How many marbles did I have?
4 X 2	5 X 2	3 X 3
4 X 3	6 X 2	7 X 3
5 X 7	2 X 9	8 X 3
2 X 2	4 X 4	5 x 5

Standard: Math I Operations & Algebraic Thinking I 3.OA.1   ©www.CoreCommonStandards.com

Name: _____

Match the Product

Directions: For the multiplication equations below, match to the correct array, multiple addition, or picture that illustrates the product.

5 X 4

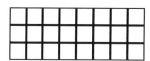

3 X 7

2 X 8

$5 + 5 + 5 + 5 + 5 =$

5 X 5

☒☒☒☒☒
☒☒☒☒☒
☒☒☒☒☒
☒☒☒☒☒

8 X 3

9 X 2

$7 + 7 + 7 =$

7 X 1

☒☒☒☒☒☒☒

Standard: Math I Operations & Algebraic Thinking I 3.OA.1   ©www.CoreCommonStandards.com

Name: _____

Show the Quotient

Directions: For the division equations below, show equal shares, draw a picture, or write a number story to illustrate the quotient.

12 ÷ 4	12 ÷ 4	12 ÷ 4
		I had twelve carrots. I gave each of my 4 rabbits an equal share of the carrots. How many carrots did each rabbit get?
16 ÷ 4	24 ÷ 8	32 ÷ 2
45 ÷ 9	20 ÷ 2	66 ÷ 11
38 ÷ 2	50 ÷ 5	63 ÷ 3
9 ÷ 1	56 ÷ 8	49 ÷ 7

Standard: Math I Operations & Algebraic Thinking I 3.OA.2   ©www.CoreCommonStandards.com

Name: _____

Match the Quotient

Directions: For the division equations below, match to the correct equal shares or picture that illustrates the quotient.

8 ÷ 2

16 ÷ 4

20 ÷ 5

40 ÷ 10

28 ÷ 4

36 ÷ 12

25 ÷ 5

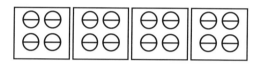

Name: _____

Multiplying Number Stories

Directions: Solve the multiplication problems. You may use drawings and equations to show your work.

Sharon went to the store 5 times for her mom. Each time she went, Sharon bought 16 potatoes. How many potatoes did Sharon buy altogether?

_____ potatoes

_____ x _____ = _____

For the 3rd grade play, we had to arrange chairs so the audience could sit. We placed the chairs in 7 rows, with 12 chairs in each row. How many chairs will there be for the play?

_____ chairs

_____ x _____ = _____

Grandma gave each of her grandkids a goody bag. Each bag held 8 pieces of candy. Grandma has 6 children. How many pieces of candy were there in all?

_____ pieces of candy

_____ x _____ = _____

The kindergarteners each wrote a book today. Each book has 8 pages. There are 11 kindergarteners in the class. How many pages did they write in all?

_____ pages

_____ x _____ = _____

Moo-Moo Farm has 25 cows. Each cow has 4 legs. How many cow legs are on the farm?

_____ cow legs

_____ x _____ = _____

Name: _____

Dividing Number Stories

Directions: Solve the division problems. You may use drawings and equations to show your work.

Sheila baked 90 cookies for the bake sale. She placed equal amounts into 15 bags. How many cookies were in each bag?

_____ cookies

_____ ÷ _____ = _____

Chef Albertine cooked 100 large raviolis. She placed 5 raviolis on each plate. How many plates did Chef use?

_____ plates

_____ ÷ _____ = _____

Connie brought 72 balloons to the party. She bundled the balloons into groups of 6. How many bundles of balloons did Connie create?

_____ bundles of balloons

_____ ÷ _____ = _____

Goober McCoy has 42 sheep that he keeps in pens. Each pen has an equal amount of sheep. There are 6 pens in the farm. How many sheep are in each pen?

_____ sheep in each pen

_____ ÷ _____ = _____

Clyde has 99 potato wedges in 9 bowls. Each bowl has the same number of potato wedges. How many wedges are in each bowl?

_____ potato wedges

_____ ÷ _____ = _____

Standard: Math l Operations & Algebraic Thinking l 3.OA.3   ©www.CoreCommonStandards.com

Name: _____

Make it True

Directions: Read the equations below. What missing number makes the equations true? Write the missing numbers into the equations.

$$13 \times \underline{\ 5\ } = 65 \qquad\qquad 72 \div 6 = \underline{\ 12\ }$$

1.	$5 \times 5 = \underline{\quad}$	11.	$45 \div 9 = \underline{\quad}$
2.	$12 \times \underline{\quad} = 36$	12.	$36 \div 6 = \underline{\quad}$
3.	$\underline{\quad} \times 8 = 88$	13.	$\underline{\quad} \div 4 = 7$
4.	$\underline{\quad} = 2 \times 50$	14.	$48 \div \underline{\quad} = 8$
5.	$45 = \underline{\quad} \times 9$	15.	$10 = \underline{\quad} \div 9$
6.	$8 \times 8 = \underline{\quad}$	16.	$\underline{\quad} = 60 \div 5$
7.	$11 \times \underline{\quad} = 88$	17.	$\underline{\quad} \div 2 = 24$
8.	$\underline{\quad} \times 7 = 63$	18.	$100 \div 25 = \underline{\quad}$
9.	$100 = 10 \times \underline{\quad}$	19.	$\underline{\quad} = 35 \div 7$
10.	$8 \times 9 = \underline{\quad}$	20.	$\underline{\quad} = 77 \div 11$

Standard: Math I Operations & Algebraic Thinking I 3.OA.4

Name: _____

Find the Missing Number

Directions: Read the equations below. What missing number makes the equations true? Write the missing numbers into the equations.

$$5 \times \underline{\ 5\ } = 25 \qquad\qquad 60 \div \underline{\ 10\ } = 6$$

1.	$3 \times 5 = \underline{\quad}$	11.	$36 \div 9 = \underline{\quad}$
2.	$10 \times \underline{\quad} = 60$	12.	$36 \div 12 = \underline{\quad}$
3.	$\underline{\quad} \times 4 = 12$	13.	$\underline{\quad} \div 8 = 5$
4.	$\underline{\quad} = 4 \times 25$	14.	$40 \div \underline{\quad} = 4$
5.	$28 = \underline{\quad} \times 7$	15.	$5 = \underline{\quad} \div 2$
6.	$5 \times 5 = \underline{\quad}$	16.	$\underline{\quad} = 50 \div 5$
7.	$11 \times \underline{\quad} = 55$	17.	$\underline{\quad} \div 2 = 12$
8.	$\underline{\quad} \times 9 = 63$	18.	$48 \div 6 = \underline{\quad}$
9.	$45 = 5 \times \underline{\quad}$	19.	$\underline{\quad} = 35 \div 5$
10.	$12 \times 4 = \underline{\quad}$	20.	$\underline{\quad} = 22 \div 11$

Standard: Math I Operations & Algebraic Thinking I 3.OA.4   ©www.CoreCommonStandards.com

Name: _____

Color the Unknown Number

Directions: Solve the multiplication and division equations below. Use the key to color the rectangular spaces with the correct colors.

Use the colors below for the answer you wrote...

| 5 - blue | 8 - orange | 10 - green |
| 6 - red | 9 - purple | 12 - yellow |

36 ÷ 6 = _____	45 ÷ 9 = _____	100 ÷ 10 = _____
5 x _____ = 25	80 ÷ _____ = 8	60 ÷ _____ = 5
3 x _____ = 27	100 ÷ 20 = _____	32 ÷ 4 = _____
3 x _____ = 30	10 = 80 ÷ _____	63 ÷ 7 = _____
1 x 12 = _____	5 x _____ = 30	3 x _____ = 36
88 ÷ 11 = _____	35 ÷ 7 = _____	4 x 2 = _____
90 ÷ 9 = _____	1 x 5 = _____	_____ = 4 x 3
72 ÷ 12 = _____	3 x 3 = _____	_____ x 10 = 60

Standard: Math I Operations & Algebraic Thinking I 3.OA.4   ©www.CoreCommonStandards.com

Name: _____

Color the Missing Number

Directions: Solve the multiplication and division equations below. Use the key to color the rectangular spaces with the correct colors.

Use the colors below for the answer you wrote...

| 4 - red | 6 - orange | 8 - green |
| 5 - blue | 7 - purple | 9 - yellow |

$28 \div 4 =$ _____	$40 \div 8 =$ _____	$80 \div 10 =$ _____
$6 \times$ _____ $= 30$	$24 \div$ _____ $= 6$	$36 \div$ _____ $= 6$
$11 \times$ _____ $= 88$	$55 \div 11 =$ _____	$18 \div 3 =$ _____
$3 \times$ _____ $= 21$	$10 = 40 \div$ _____	$16 \div 2 =$ _____
$3 \times 3 =$ _____	$7 \times$ _____ $= 49$	$3 \times$ _____ $= 27$
$32 \div 4 =$ _____	$81 \div 9 =$ _____	$2 \times 3 =$ _____
$10 \div 2 =$ _____	$2 \times 2 =$ _____	_____ $= 4 \times 2$
$64 \div 8 =$ _____	$42 \div 6 =$ _____	_____ $\times 6 = 54$

Standard: Math I Operations & Algebraic Thinking I 3.OA.4   ©www.CoreCommonStandards.com

Name: _____

Multiplying with Strategies

Directions: Solve the multiplication equations by using one of the strategies you have learned.

6x4=24 so 4x6=24 (commutative)   3x5x2 is 3x5=15 and 15x2=30 (associative)
8x7 is 8x(5+2) so (8x5) + (8x2) = 40 + 16 which is 56..so 8x7=56 (distributive)

7 x 4 = _____	3 x 5 x 4 = _____
6 x 9 = _____	8 x 5 = _____
4 x 2 x 6 = _____	10 x 4 x 1 = _____
3 x 3 x 3 = _____	12 x 5 = _____

Standard: Math I Operations & Algebraic Thinking I 3.OA.5   ©www.CoreCommonStandards.com

Level: Third Grade   Name: _____

Multiplying with Strategies

Directions: Solve the multiplication equations by using one of the strategies you have learned.

6x4=24 so 4x6=24 (commutative)   3x5x2 is 3x5=15 and 15x2=30 (associative)
8x7 is 8x(5+2) so (8x5) + (8x2) = 40 + 16 which is 56..so 8x7=56 (distributive)

12 x 7 = _____	4 x 25 = _____
10 x 9 x 1 = _____	2 x 37 = _____
45 x 2 = _____	8 x 2 x 4 = _____
48 x 2 = _____	13 x 5 x 1 = _____

Standard: Math I Operations & Algebraic Thinking I 3.OA.5   ©www.CoreCommonStandards.com

Name: _____

Match the Fact Families

Directions: Match the division equations on the left to the multiplication equations on the right that share a common factor and are in the same fact family.

$16 \div 2$	9×7
$20 \div 4$	5×5
$25 \div 5$	8×2
$60 \div 10$	16×4
$28 \div 4$	12×3
$36 \div 12$	4×5
$45 \div 5$	4×7
$64 \div 16$	5×9
$63 \div 9$	10×6

Standard: Math I Operations & Algebraic Thinking I 3.OA.6   ©www.CoreCommonStandards.com

Name: _____

Match the Fact Families

Directions: Match the division equations on the left to the multiplication equations on the right that share a common factor and are in the same fact family.

$21 \div 7$	4×10
$24 \div 8$	3×8
$30 \div 5$	6×7
$40 \div 10$	3×7
$12 \div 4$	7×7
$33 \div 11$	6×5
$42 \div 7$	3×4
$64 \div 8$	3×11
$49 \div 7$	8×8

Standard: Math I Operations & Algebraic Thinking I 3.OA.6

Name: _____

Multiplying Within One Hundred

Directions: Solve the multiplication equations by using one of the strategies you have learned.

$9 \times 6 =$	$8 \times 4 =$	$5 \times 4 =$	$9 \times 9 =$
$7 \times 4 =$	$3 \times 6 =$	$6 \times 8 =$	$4 \times 1 =$
$6 \times 6 =$	$5 \times 3 =$	$5 \times 8 =$	$7 \times 2 =$
$5 \times 5 =$	$4 \times 8 =$	$3 \times 7 =$	$8 \times 7 =$
$\begin{array}{r} 8 \\ \times\ 8 \\ \hline \end{array}$	$\begin{array}{r} 3 \\ \times\ 4 \\ \hline \end{array}$	$\begin{array}{r} 6 \\ \times\ 5 \\ \hline \end{array}$	$\begin{array}{r} 4 \\ \times\ 4 \\ \hline \end{array}$
$\begin{array}{r} 7 \\ \times\ 2 \\ \hline \end{array}$	$\begin{array}{r} 6 \\ \times\ 1 \\ \hline \end{array}$	$\begin{array}{r} 5 \\ \times\ 3 \\ \hline \end{array}$	$\begin{array}{r} 4 \\ \times\ 5 \\ \hline \end{array}$

Standard: Math I Operations & Algebraic Thinking I 3.OA.7   ©www.CoreCommonStandards.com

Name: _____

That's A Fact

<u>Directions:</u> Solve the multiplication and division equations in each house. Do you notice a pattern?

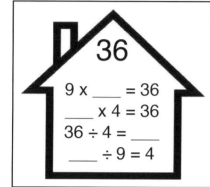

36

9 x ___ = 36
___ x 4 = 36
36 ÷ 4 = ___
___ ÷ 9 = 4

45

9 x ___ = 45
___ x 9 = 45
45 ÷ 5 = ___
___ ÷ 9 = 5

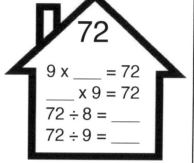

72

9 x ___ = 72
___ x 9 = 72
72 ÷ 8 = ___
72 ÷ 9 = ___

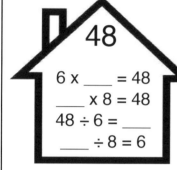

48

6 x ___ = 48
___ x 8 = 48
48 ÷ 6 = ___
___ ÷ 8 = 6

30

5 x ___ = 30
___ x 6 = 30
30 ÷ 6 = ___
___ ÷ 5 = 6

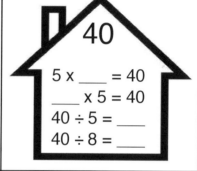

40

5 x ___ = 40
___ x 5 = 40
40 ÷ 5 = ___
40 ÷ 8 = ___

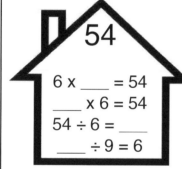

54

6 x ___ = 54
___ x 6 = 54
54 ÷ 6 = ___
___ ÷ 9 = 6

63

9 x ___ = 63
___ x 7 = 63
63 ÷ 7 = ___
___ ÷ 9 = 7

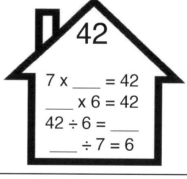

42

7 x ___ = 42
___ x 6 = 42
42 ÷ 6 = ___
___ ÷ 7 = 6

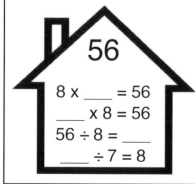

56

8 x ___ = 56
___ x 8 = 56
56 ÷ 8 = ___
___ ÷ 7 = 8

28

7 x ___ = 28
___ x 4 = 28
28 ÷ 4 = ___
28 ÷ 7 = ___

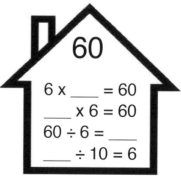

60

6 x ___ = 60
___ x 6 = 60
60 ÷ 6 = ___
___ ÷ 10 = 6

Standard: Math I Operations & Algebraic Thinking I 3.OA.7

Follow the Steps

Directions: Solve the following problems. Think about the operation (+, - , x , ÷) you can use to solve each problem. Write an equation to help you solve. Place a letter in the space of the unknown quantity. ex: $45 \div a = 9$

Paulette wanted to give all of her Easter candy to her 7 cousins. She had 91 pieces of candy. She made sure each cousin had the same amount. How much candy did each cousin get?

_____ pieces

Borsch the Baker needed eggs to bake his cake. He asked his assistant, Juniper, to buy 5 dozen eggs. How many eggs did Juniper buy?

_____ eggs

Pablo has 20 cupcakes for his friends. Each cupcake has 4 candles. Susie secretly stuck 3 more into her cupcake. How many candles are on the cupcakes?

_____ candles

The 21 children in Mrs. Poppasquash's class each held 4 tulips for a class picture. Before the picture was taken, 3 of Karen's tulips were stolen by a bird. How many tulips made it into the picture?

_____ tulips

Each pack of crayons had 24 crayons. Betty and her 2 sisters, Eliza and Carmen, each received a pack for Christmas. By the end of the day, Betty broke 2 crayons, Eliza lost 3, and Carmen ate 1. How many crayons were left at the end of the day?

_____ crayons

Name: _____

Following the Steps

Directions: Solve the following problems. Think about the operation (+, - , x , ÷) you can use to solve each problem. Write an equation to help you solve. Place a letter in the space of the unknown quantity. ex: $45 ÷ a = 9$

Kyle has 37 Matchbox cars. Harry has 43. How many more Matchbox cars does Harry have then Kyle?

_____ cars

If Kyle and Harry combine their cars into one group and split them equally in half, how many cars would each child get?

_____ cars

George ordered 7 pizzas for the party. Each pizza has 8 slices. 50 people were invited to the party. How many extra slices of pizza will there be?

_____ slices

If George's daughters, Mary and Lu-Lu, equally share the remaining slices, how many slices will they each get to eat?

_____ slices

The clothing store just received a new shipment of ties. There are 20 blue ties, 14 red ties, and 36 polka-dot ties. How many ties arrived at the store?

_____ ties

If half of the ties go out onto the sale floor, and half stay in the back, how many ties will be out on the floor?

_____ ties

Kathy has 5 times as many pennies as Frank. Frank has 16 pennies. How many pennies does Kathy have?

_____ pennies

Kathy bought a bouncy ball for 36¢. How much money does Kathy have now?

_____ cents

Standard: Math I Operations & Algebraic Thinking I 3.OA.8   ©www.CoreCommonStandards.com

Name: _____

Find the Patterns

Directions: Complete the addition table below. Look for patterns in the table. Use colored pencils to circle patterns you see. Explain to someone what patterns you noticed.

+	0	1	2	3	4	5	6	7	8	9
0										
1										
2										
3										
4										
5										
6										
7										
8										
9										

What patterns do you notice?

Name: _____

Find the Patterns

Directions: Complete the multiplication table below. Look for patterns in the table. Use colored pencils to circle patterns you see. Explain to someone what patterns you noticed.

x	0	1	2	3	4	5	6	7	8	9
0										
1										
2										
3										
4										
5										
6										
7										
8										
9										

What patterns do you notice?

Standard: Math I Operations & Algebraic Thinking I 3.OA.9   ©www.CoreCommonStandards.com

Name: _____

What's the Rule?

Directions: Look for the patterns in the Addition/Subtraction In/Out boxes below. Write the rule that applies to each box.

rule	in	out
	1	6
	2	7
	3	8
	4	9
	5	10

rule	in	out
	1	9
	2	10
	3	11
	4	12
	5	13

rule	in	out
	2	32
	3	33
	5	35
	6	36
	8	38

rule	in	out
	4	29
	6	31
	9	34
	10	35
	12	37

rule	in	out
	50	40
	35	25
	25	15
	10	0
	40	30

rule	in	out
	14	5
	28	19
	42	31
	77	68
	49	40

rule	in	out
	16	8
	20	12
	32	24
	40	32
	48	40

rule	in	out
	44	24
	60	40
	100	80
	55	35
	87	67

rule	in	out
	33	26
	47	40
	94	87
	12	5
	39	32

Standard: Math l Operations & Algebraic Thinking l 3.OA.9   ©www.CoreCommonStandards.com

Name: _____

What's the Rule?

Directions: Look for the patterns in the Multiplication/Division In/Out boxes below. Write the rule that applies to each box.

rule		in	out
		1	3
		2	6
		3	9
		4	12
		5	15

rule		in	out
		1	5
		2	10
		3	15
		4	20
		5	25

rule		in	out
		2	16
		3	24
		5	40
		6	48
		8	64

rule		in	out
		4	36
		6	54
		9	81
		10	90
		12	108

rule		in	out
		50	10
		35	7
		25	5
		10	2
		40	8

rule		in	out
		14	2
		28	4
		42	6
		77	11
		49	7

rule		in	out
		16	4
		20	5
		32	8
		40	10
		48	12

rule		in	out
		8	8
		22	22
		45	45
		61	61
		87	87

rule		in	out
		30	3
		40	4
		70	7
		90	9
		100	10

Standard: Math I Operations & Algebraic Thinking I 3.OA.9   ©www.CoreCommonStandards.com

Name: _____

Round to Nearest Ten

Directions: Match the number on the hook to the fish rounded to the nearest 10.

 55

 70

 43

 30

 72

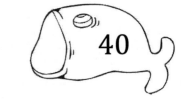 40

 87

 90

 29

 60

 34

 30

Standard: Math I Number & Operations in Base Ten I 3.NBT.1

Name: _____

Round to Nearest Hundred

Directions: Match the number on the spoon to the sundae rounded to the nearest 100.

 236

 600

 300

719

 200

283

420

 400

575

 900

867

 700

Standard: Math I Number & Operations in Base Ten I 3.NBT.1   ©www.CoreCommonStandards.com

Level: Third Grade   Name: _____

Adding To One Thousand

Directions: Add the Ones, Tens, and Hundreds below. Use the strategies you have learned to help you.

$$344 + 366$$ $$456 + 284$$ $$294 + 692$$ $$482 + 235$$

$$449 + 326$$ $$249 + 427$$ $$277 + 415$$ $$802 + 100$$

433 + 227 = ☐   545 + 317 = ☐

208 + 340 = ☐   209 + 749 = ☐

197 + 765 = ☐   642 + 108 = ☐

335 + 464 = ☐   720 + 279 = ☐

Standard: Math I Number & Operations in Base Ten I 3.NBT.2   ©www.CoreCommonStandards.com

Name: _____

Subtraction From One Thousand

<u>Directions:</u> Subtract the Ones, Tens and Hundreds below. Use the strategies you have learned to help you.

945	725	980	914
-153	- 244	- 279	- 753

854	946	987	827
- 375	- 625	- 415	- 715

827 - 252 = ☐   879 - 317 = ☐

915 - 520 = ☐   902 - 429 = ☐

815 - 255 = ☐   658 - 158 = ☐

726 - 264 = ☐   925 - 456 = ☐

Name: _____

Multiplying by Multiples of Ten

Directions: Solve the multiplication equations by using one of the strategies you have learned.

30 x 4 =	50 x 5 =	40 x 4 =	10 x 10 =
20 x 4 =	3 x 50 =	6 x 70 =	90 x 1 =
6 x 30 =	50 x 1 =	20 x 8 =	60 x 4 =
50 x 2 =	40 x 9 =	70 x 2 =	90 x 7 =
50 x 8	70 x 4	10 x 5	80 x 4
80 x 2	60 x 9	40 x 5	90 x 5

Standard: Math I Number & Operations in Base Ten I 3.NBT.3   ©www.CoreCommonStandards.com

Name: _____

Matching Multiplication

Directions: Match the multiplication equation on the left to the correct product on the right.

equation	product
a. 40 x 3 =	_____ 320
b. 70 x 4 =	_____ 400
c. 3 x 90 =	_____ 250
d. 50 x 3 =	_____ 120
e. 40 x 8 =	_____ 360
f. 50 x 5 =	_____ 140
g. 80 x 5 =	_____ 270
h. 6 x 30 =	_____ 630
i. 9 x 10 =	_____ 120
j. 4 x 30 =	_____ 250
k. 5 x 50 =	_____ 280
l. 9 x 50 =	_____ 180
m. 90 x 7 =	_____ 450
n. 70 x 3 =	_____ 90
o. 20 x 7 =	_____ 210
p. 60 x 6 =	_____ 150

Standard: Math I Number & Operations in Base Ten I 3.NBT.3   ©www.CoreCommonStandards.com

Name: _____

Pizza Fractions

Directions: Look at the shaded slices. Circle the correct fraction for each pizza.

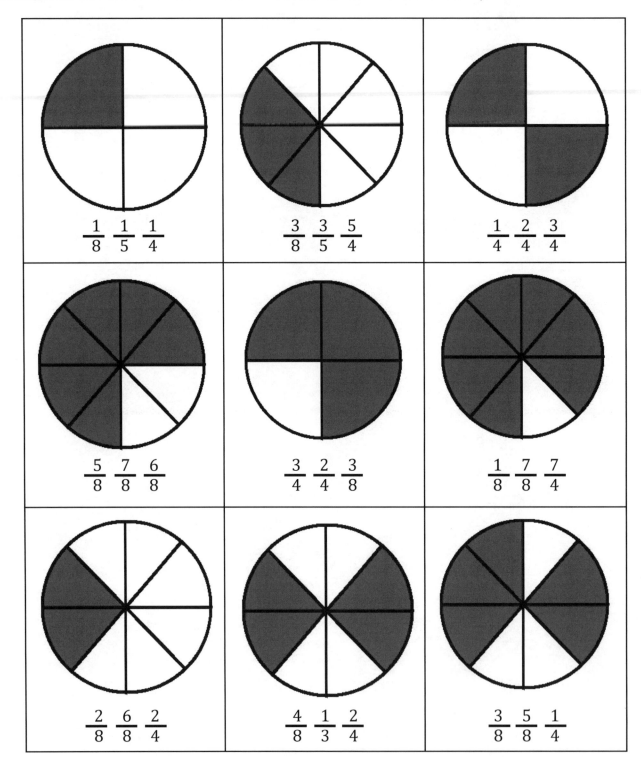

$\dfrac{1}{8}$ $\dfrac{1}{5}$ $\dfrac{1}{4}$

$\dfrac{3}{8}$ $\dfrac{3}{5}$ $\dfrac{5}{4}$

$\dfrac{1}{4}$ $\dfrac{2}{4}$ $\dfrac{3}{4}$

$\dfrac{5}{8}$ $\dfrac{7}{8}$ $\dfrac{6}{8}$

$\dfrac{3}{4}$ $\dfrac{2}{4}$ $\dfrac{3}{8}$

$\dfrac{1}{8}$ $\dfrac{7}{8}$ $\dfrac{7}{4}$

$\dfrac{2}{8}$ $\dfrac{6}{8}$ $\dfrac{2}{4}$

$\dfrac{4}{8}$ $\dfrac{1}{3}$ $\dfrac{2}{4}$

$\dfrac{3}{8}$ $\dfrac{5}{8}$ $\dfrac{1}{4}$

Standard: Math I Number & Operations-Fractions I 3.NF.1   ©www.CoreCommonStandards.com

Name: _____

Rectangle Fractions

Directions: Look at the shaded parts. Circle the correct fraction for each rectangle.

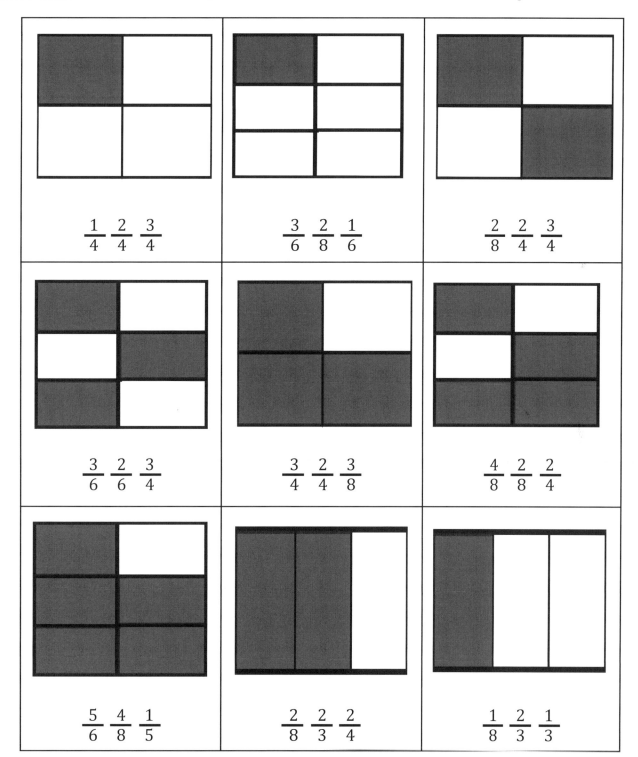

$\dfrac{1}{4}$ $\dfrac{2}{4}$ $\dfrac{3}{4}$

$\dfrac{3}{6}$ $\dfrac{2}{8}$ $\dfrac{1}{6}$

$\dfrac{2}{8}$ $\dfrac{2}{4}$ $\dfrac{3}{4}$

$\dfrac{3}{6}$ $\dfrac{2}{6}$ $\dfrac{3}{4}$

$\dfrac{3}{4}$ $\dfrac{2}{4}$ $\dfrac{3}{8}$

$\dfrac{4}{8}$ $\dfrac{2}{8}$ $\dfrac{2}{4}$

$\dfrac{5}{6}$ $\dfrac{4}{8}$ $\dfrac{1}{5}$

$\dfrac{2}{8}$ $\dfrac{2}{3}$ $\dfrac{2}{4}$

$\dfrac{1}{8}$ $\dfrac{2}{3}$ $\dfrac{1}{3}$

Standard: Math I Number & Operations-Fractions I 3.NF.1   ©www.CoreCommonStandards.com

Name: _____

Number Line Fractions

Directions: Circle the fraction that is marked in red on the number line.

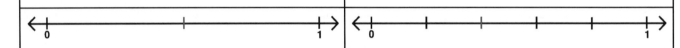 $\frac{1}{3}$ $\frac{2}{3}$ $\frac{2}{4}$	$\frac{1}{4}$ $\frac{2}{4}$ $\frac{1}{5}$
$\frac{1}{3}$ $\frac{1}{2}$ $\frac{2}{3}$	$\frac{2}{4}$ $\frac{2}{3}$ $\frac{2}{5}$
$\frac{3}{3}$ $\frac{2}{3}$ $\frac{3}{4}$	$\frac{1}{2}$ $\frac{2}{4}$ $\frac{1}{6}$
$\frac{1}{3}$ $\frac{2}{3}$ $\frac{1}{4}$	$\frac{2}{5}$ $\frac{2}{3}$ $\frac{2}{4}$
$\frac{1}{5}$ $\frac{1}{6}$ $\frac{2}{6}$	$\frac{1}{3}$ $\frac{1}{5}$ $\frac{2}{4}$

Standard: Math I Numbers & Operations-Fractions I 3.NF.2   ©www.CoreCommonStandards.com

Name: _____

Number Line Fractions

Directions: Circle the fraction that is marked in red on the number line.

$\dfrac{1}{6}$ $\dfrac{4}{6}$ $\dfrac{2}{5}$	$\dfrac{1}{6}$ $\dfrac{4}{7}$ $\dfrac{3}{7}$
$\dfrac{1}{8}$ $\dfrac{3}{9}$ $\dfrac{5}{9}$	$\dfrac{6}{9}$ $\dfrac{4}{7}$ $\dfrac{7}{9}$
$\dfrac{4}{7}$ $\dfrac{2}{7}$ $\dfrac{3}{7}$	$\dfrac{6}{8}$ $\dfrac{4}{9}$ $\dfrac{5}{8}$
$\dfrac{4}{8}$ $\dfrac{3}{9}$ $\dfrac{5}{8}$	$\dfrac{2}{6}$ $\dfrac{4}{8}$ $\dfrac{3}{6}$
$\dfrac{6}{8}$ $\dfrac{4}{9}$ $\dfrac{3}{9}$	$\dfrac{6}{10}$ $\dfrac{7}{10}$ $\dfrac{5}{10}$

Standard: Math | Numbers & Operations-Fractions | 3.NF.2   ©www.CoreCommonStandards.com

Name: _____

Placing Fractions on a Number Line

Directions: Locate the fraction on the number. Color a dot on the number line to show the fraction.

$\dfrac{1}{1}$	$\dfrac{1}{2}$
$\dfrac{2}{3}$	$\dfrac{3}{4}$
$\dfrac{3}{5}$	$\dfrac{4}{6}$
$\dfrac{5}{7}$	$\dfrac{2}{8}$
$\dfrac{7}{9}$	$\dfrac{6}{10}$

Standard: Math I Numbers & Operations-Fractions I 3.NF.2   ©www.CoreCommonStandards.com

Name: _____

Placing Fractions on a Number Line

Directions: Choose a fraction to write on the blank line. Then, color a dot on the number line to show the fraction.

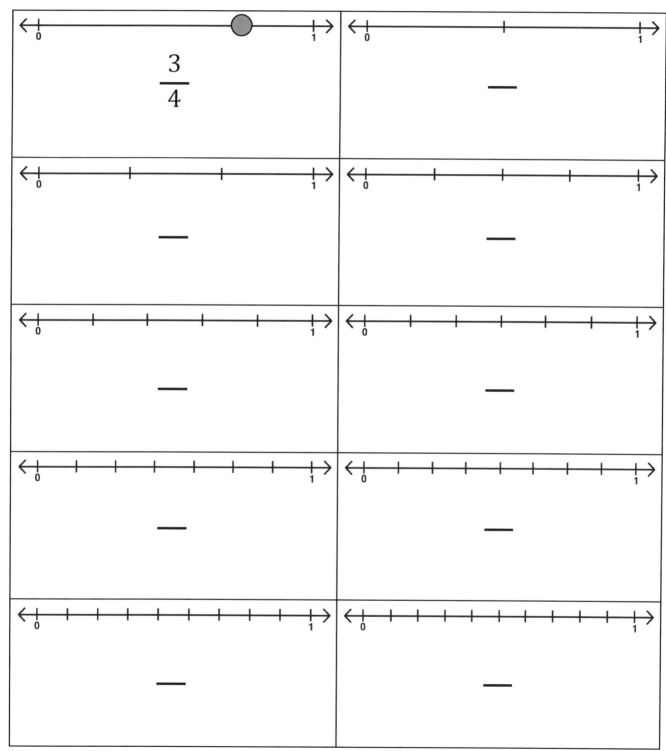

Standard: Math I Numbers & Operations-Fractions I 3.NF.2   ©www.CoreCommonStandards.com

Name: _____

Matching Equivalents

Directions: Read the fraction on the left. Circle its correct equivalent fraction on the right.

Fraction	Equivalent		
2/6	4/5	1/3	2/4
4/8	5/6	1/2	7/8
5/15	1/3	7/9	3/6
7/14	9/10	6/8	1/2
3/12	1/4	4/8	3/8
8/10	4/5	6/8	3/9
5/20	1/9	1/4	7/20
2/16	2/8	5/8	1/8
7/21	1/3	3/7	8/16
6/10	3/5	8/9	5/8
12/18	4/5	2/3	4/7
12/20	3/5	8/9	2/8
10/30	4/16	7/8	1/3
4/10	4/5	2/5	3/5
8/12	1/3	2/3	4/5
9/27	1/2	1/3	1/9

Standard: Math I Number & Operations-FractionsI 3.NF.3   ©www.CoreCommonStandards.com

Name: _____

One of These Does NOT Belong!

Directions: Read the fraction on the left. Circle the answer on the right that is **NOT** a correct equivalent fraction.

Fraction	Which is NOT equivalent?		
1/2	2/4	3/6	5/9
1/3	1/6	3/9	4/12
1/4	2/8	3/11	3/12
1/5	2/10	3/15	4/25
1/6	3/12	3/18	4/24
2/3	4/6	8/12	12/20
2/4	3/8	4/8	5/10
2/5	4/10	6/15	8/18
2/6	1/3	4/9	4/12
3/4	1/3	6/8	9/12
3/5	6/11	6/10	9/15
3/6	1/2	2/4	4/9
4/5	8/10	12/16	16/20
4/6	3/4	2/3	12/18
5/6	10/12	15/18	20/22

Standard: Math | Number & Operations-Fractions| 3.NF.3   ©www.CoreCommonStandards.com

Name: _____

What Time is It?

Directions: Look at the clocks below. What time is it? Write the digital times beneath the clocks.
Then, calculate the new elapsed time by adding the minutes in the gray boxes. Draw the new hands
and write the new digital time.

(clock)	add 15 minutes	(clock)	add 10 minutes	(clock)
(clock)	add 20 minutes	(clock)	add 25 minutes	(clock)
(clock)	add 43 minutes	(clock)	add 51 minutes	(clock)
(clock)	add 16 minutes	(clock)	add 32 minutes	(clock)

Standard: Math I Measurement & Data I 3.MD.1   ©www.CoreCommonStandards.com

Level: Third Grade

Name: _____

Elapsed Time Stories

Directions: Read the number stories below. Calculate the elapsed time for each story. You can use the clocks to help you solve.

Marianne began her homework at 3:20 pm. She finished it at 4:45 pm. How long did it take Marianne to complete her homework?

_____ hour _____minutes

The movie started at 6:11pm. It lasted 84 minutes. At what time did the movie finish?

_____ pm

It takes Frank 47 minutes to get from his house to the store. If he wants to be at the store at 9:00 am, what time does Frank need to leave his house?

_____ am

Nemo started his Facetime conversation with Dory at 4:35 pm. They finally said goodbye at 8:22 pm. How long did the two friends speak?

_____ hours _____ minutes

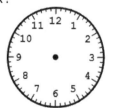 

Betty Spaghetti spent 1 hour and 23 minutes making spaghetti, and 1 hour and 40 minutes making meatballs. How long did Betty take to make the dinner?

_____ hours _____ minutes

Standard: Math l Measurement & Data l 3.MD.1

©www.CoreCommonStandards.com

Name: _____

Density and Volume in Metric

Directions: Circle the best measurement unit {liters, milliliters, grams, or kilograms} for each object below.

the volume of a bottle of nail polish	the weight of a walnut	the volume of a bottle of soda
grams kilograms liters milliliters	grams kilograms liters milliliters	grams kilograms liters milliliters
the weight of a duck	the volume of water in a fish bowl	the volume of a dose of cough medicine
grams kilograms liters milliliters	grams kilograms liters milliliters	grams kilograms liters milliliters
the weight of a paper clip	the volume of a tank of gasoline	the weight of an elephant
grams kilograms liters milliliters	grams kilograms liters milliliters	grams kilograms liters milliliters
the weight of a feather	the volume of a teaspoon of vanilla	the weight of an automobile
grams kilograms liters milliliters	grams kilograms liters milliliters	grams kilograms liters milliliters

Standard: Math | Measurement & Data | 3.MD.2

Name: _____

Measuring Volume and Mass

Directions: Solve the metric problems. You may use drawings and equations to show your work.

Brandy needed to bake 5 cakes for a party. She followed the recipe for one cake and multiplied by 5 to increase the ingredients. The recipe called for 34 grams of sugar. How many grams of sugar was needed for 5 cakes?

_____ grams

Paul had 3 plastic bags with 150 milliliters of water. Each bag had a fish. When he poured all of the bags of water into a bowl, how many milliliters of water were in the bowl?

_____ milliliters

Susan's cat weighed 4 kilograms. Bob's cat weighed 5 kg. Mary's cat weighed 6 kg. Gary was waiting to weigh his cat. Altogether, the cats weighed 20 kg. How much did Gary's cat weigh?

_____ kilograms

Henrietta won a chocolate bar that weighed 1815 grams, (or 4 pounds). She shared the candy bar equally with two of her friends. How many grams of chocolate did each of the three friends get to eat?

_____ grams

Mom asked me to buy 18 bottles of soda for the graduation party. Each bottle contained 2 liters of liquid. One bottle fell and when I opened it, it exploded. How many liters of soda did we end up with for the party?

_____ liters

Standard: Math I Measurement & Data I 3.MD.2   ©www.CoreCommonStandards.com

Name: _____

Make a Pictograph Using Data

<u>Directions:</u> Read the problem below. Create a pictograph that will represent the data. Answer the question by using the graph.

Carlo and Nina took a survey of their schoolmates to see what their favorite cotton-candy flavor is. The results are listed below.

Fruity-Tooty - 35   **Licorice - 25**   **Root Beer - 40**

Strawberry - 40   **Bubblegum - 10**

Flavor	Number of Votes	KEY
Fruity-Tooty		
Strawberry		
Licorice		
Bubblegum		
Root Beer		

1. What was the total of the two favorite cotton-candy flavors?

2. How many more students voted for Fruity-Tooty than Licorice?

3. How many students voted in all?

4. How many times more did students vote for Root Beer than Bubble Gum?

Standard: Math l Measurement & Data l 3.MD.3   ©www.CoreCommonStandards.com

Name: _____

Make a Pictograph Using Data

Directions: Read the problem below. Create a pictograph that will represent the data. Answer
the question by using the graph.

**Harold and his four friends, Luke, Myron, Carl, and Gabe, collected stamps. They
preserved their stamps in books that held 12 stamps. Below are the number of books
each boy had.**

Luke -   4 books   **Harold - 5 books**   **Carl - 5 1/2 books**

Myron - 3 books   **Gabe - 3 books**

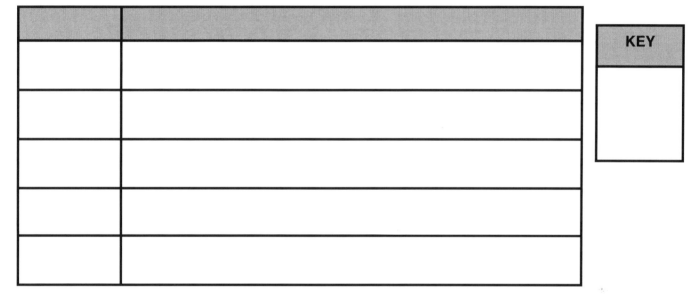

1. How many stamps did Luke collect?

2. How many more stamps did Carl collect than Myron?

3. How many stamps were collected in all?

4. How stamps did Harold and Gabe collect?

Standard: Math I Measurement & Data I 3.MD.3   ©www.CoreCommonStandards.com

Name: _____

Graphing Measurements

<u>Directions:</u> Measure each of the objects below. Use the measurements to create a line graph on page 2.

1.

_____ inches

2.

_____ inches

3.

_____ inches

4.

_____ inches

5.

_____ inches

6.

_____ inches

Standard: Math I Measurement & Data I 3.MD.4   ©www.CoreCommonStandards.com

Name: _____

Measurements From Page 1

1. _____ in   2. _____ in   3. _____ in
4. _____ in   5. _____ in   6. _____ in

Name: _____

Graphing Measurements

Directions: Measure each of the objects below. Use the measurements to create a line graph on page 2. (If you don't have time, make up your own numbers in the chart below that show growth over time)

Materials:

cup
soil
water
kidney or lima bean
inch ruler (with 1/2 in
and 1/4 in)

Procedure:

Plant a kidney bean or lima bean into soil.
Add Water.
Observe the seed's growth each day.
Record its growth in inches on the chart below.

Day	Height	Growth
ex: day 5 ex: day 15	1 in 5 in	1 in 4 in
day 1		
day 5		
day 8		
day 12		
day 15		
day 18		
day 20		

Name: _____

Use the data above about your plant's growth and create a line graph that shows its growth over time.

What can you say about the growth of your plant?

Measuring Unit Squares

Directions: Find the area, I in unit squares, by counting the squares in each object.

1.

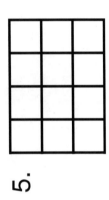

Area = _____

2.

Area = _____

3.

Area = _____

4.

Area = _____

5.

Area = _____

6.

Area = _____

7.

Area = _____

8.

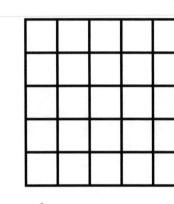

Area = _____

Standard: Mathematics I Measurement and Data I 3.MD.5

Finding the Area in Total Units

Directions: Count the number of same-size squares in each shape to find the area in square units inside.

This shape has an area of

_____ units.

This shape has an area of _____ units.

This shape has an area of

_____ units.

This shape has an area of

_____ units.

This shape has an area of _____ units.

Finding the Area in Square Units

Directions: Count the number of same-size squares in each shape to find the area in square units inside.

area = _____ sq. units

area = _____ sq. units

area = _____ sq. units

area = _____ sq. units

area = _____ sq. units

area = _____ sq. units

Standard: Math I Measurement & Data I 3.MD.5   ©www.CoreCommonStandards.com

Level: Third Grade   Name: _____

Finding the Area in Square Centimeters

Directions: Count the number of same-size squares in each shape to find the area in square centimeters inside.

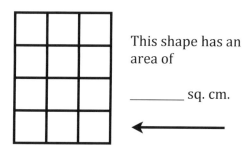

This shape has an area of

_____ sq. cm.

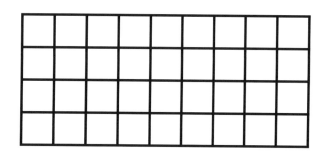

This shape has an area of _____ sq. cm.

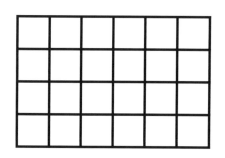

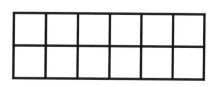

This shape has an area of _____ sq. cm.

This shape has an area of

_____ sq. cm.

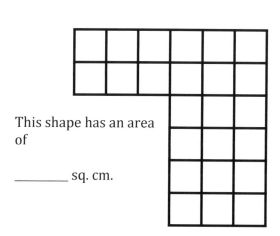

This shape has an area of

_____ sq. cm.

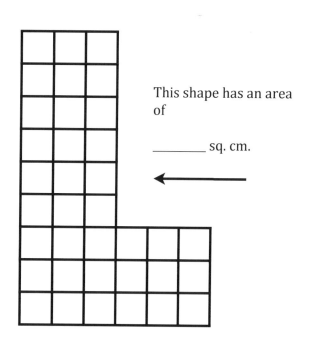

This shape has an area of

_____ sq. cm.

Standard: Math I Measurement & Data I 3.MD.6

Name: _____

Finding the Area in Square Units

Directions: Count the number of same-size squares in each shape to find the area in square centimeters, square inches, square feet, and square miles inside.

the pattern on an apron	sink tile in the bathroom	Auntie Mae's quilt
area = _____ sq. in.	area = _____ sq. cm.	area = _____ sq. in.
part of a checkerboard	kitchen floor tiles	section of a map
area = _____ sq. in.	area = _____ sq. ft.	area = _____ sq. miles

Standard: Math I Measurement & Data I 3.MD.6

©www.CoreCommonStandards.com

Finding Area by Multiplying

Directions: Find the area of each rectangle by counting the same-size squares within each shape. You can also find the area by multiplying the lengths of each side.

3

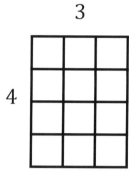

area= _____ sq. units

9

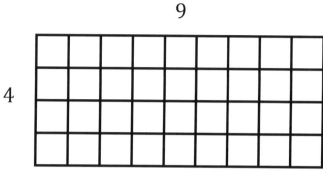

area= _____ sq. units

6

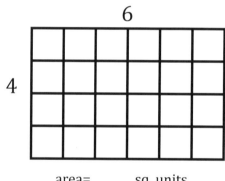

area= _____ sq. units

6

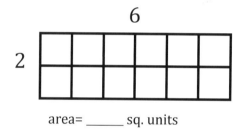

area= _____ sq. units

8

area= _____ sq. units

3

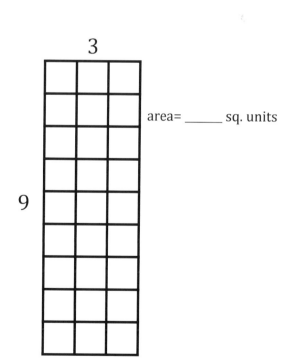

area= _____ sq. units

Standard: Math I Measurement & Data I 3.MD.7   ©www.CoreCommonStandards.com

Name: _____

Finding Area by Multiplying

Directions: Find the area of each rectangle by multiplying the lengths of each side.

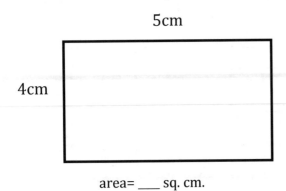

5cm

4cm

area= ___ sq. cm.

3cm

3cm

area = ___ sq. cm.

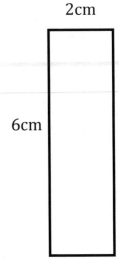

2cm

6cm

area = ___ sq. cm.

7cm

2cm

area= ___ sq. cm.

Below: Find the area for each shape, then add the two areas together.

5cm

4cm

area= ___ sq. cm.

3cm

3cm

area= ___ sq. cm.

Total Area

area= ___ sq. cm.

Standard: Math | Measurement & Data | 3.MD.7

Name: _____

Finding Perimeter

Directions: Find the perimeter of each rectangle by finding the sums of the sides. Remember that a rectangle has 2 pairs of parallel sides where opposite sides are of equal length.

3

4

Perimeter =

_____ft

7

4

Perimeter = _____ft

6

3

Perimeter = _____ft

6

7

Perimeter = _____ft

5

4

Perimeter = _____ft

Standard: Math | Measurement & Data | 3.MD.8

Name: _____

Perimeter Problems

Directions: Solve the perimeter problems. You may use drawings and equations to show your work.

Mr. Bartley wanted to build a fence around his backyard. He measured each side of his rectangular yard. The longest side measured 14 feet.   The shorter side measured 10 feet. How much fencing does Mr. Bartley need to buy to surround his yard?

_____ feet

Patty's mom wanted to put up a wallpaper border around her room.   She has exactly enough wallpaper to cover 3 walls. Wall 1 is 10 feet wide. Wall 2 is 13 feet wide. Wall 3 is 19 feet wide. The total perimeter of the room is 52 feet. How much more wallpaper border does Patty's mom need to buy to finish the 4th wall?

_____ feet

Bob's gazebo has a perimeter of 36 meters. The gazebo is a hexagon with all equal sides. How many meters long is each side of Bob's gazebo?

_____ meters

Dad bought a new TV for the living room. The measurements of the top and bottom are each 2 1/2 feet. The side measurements are each 1 1/2 feet. What it is the total perimeter of the TV?

_____ feet

Grandpa made us a new sandbox in the backyard. It has 5 sides. I measured four sides but then my ruler broke. Grandpa said the perimeter of the sandbox is 115 inches. I drew a picture to help me figure out the measurement of the last side.

_____ inches

20 in   36 in

20 in   24 in

?

Name: _____

Finding Quadrilaterals

Directions: Look at the shapes below. Color the quadrilaterals red. Can you explain why they are quadrilaterals?

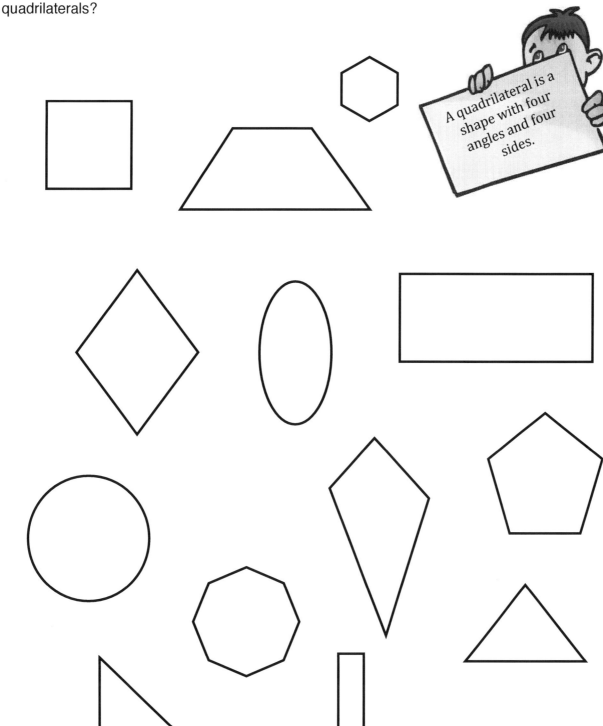

A quadrilateral is a shape with four angles and four sides.

Name: _____

Drawing Quadrilaterals

Directions: Squares, rectangles, and rhombuses are quadrilaterals. Can you draw other quadrilaterals?

Draw some different quadrilaterals below.
Name them if you can. Why are they quadrilaterals?

A quadrilateral is a shape with four angles and four sides.

Standard: Math I Geometry I 3.G.1

©www.CoreCommonStandards.com

Name: _____

Drawing Non-Quadrilaterals

Directions: Squares, rectangles, and rhombuses are quadrilaterals.
Can you draw non-quadrilaterals?

Draw some different non-quadrilaterals below.
Name them if you can. Why are they NOT quadrilaterals?

A quadrilateral is a shape with four angles and four sides.

Standard: Math I Geometry I 3.G.1

Name: _____

Fractions of a Whole

Directions: Label the fractions shaded in each figure below.

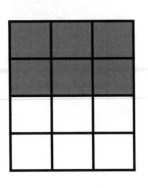   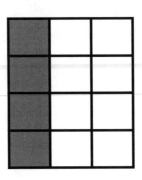   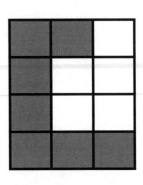

_____   _____   _____

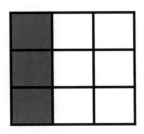   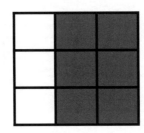   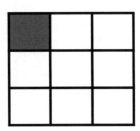

_____   _____   _____

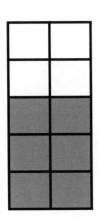   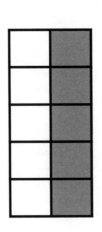   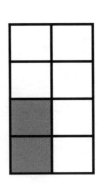   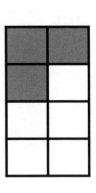

_____   _____   _____   _____

Standard: Math I Geometry I 3.G.2

Name: _____

Fractions of a Whole

Directions: Section the shapes into equal parts according to the denominator below each. Shade a portion of the shape and complete the fraction.

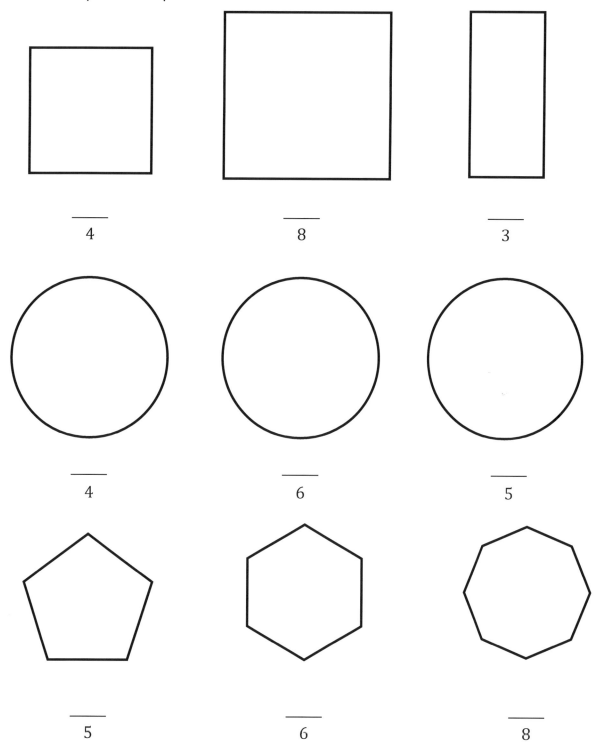

©www.CoreCommonStandards.com

 Common Core State Standards
Educating classrooms one standard at a time.

Terms of Use

All worksheets, activities, workbooks and other printable materials purchased or downloaded from this website are protected under copyright law. Items purchased from this website may be used, copied and printed for classroom, personal and home use depending on how many licenses are purchased. Upon printing and copying the materials from this website, you must leave the Copyright Information at the bottom of each item printed. Items may not be copied or distributed unless you have purchased them from this website. Furthermore, you may not reproduce, sell, or copy these resources, or post on your website any Worksheet, Activity, PDF, Workbook, or Printable without written permission from Have Fun Teaching, LLC using the contact form below. All Common Core State Standards are from CoreStandards.org and the Common Core State Standards Initiative.

All Common Core State Standards in this book are © Copyright 2010. National Governors Association Center for Best Practices and Council of Chief State School Officers. All rights reserved. Furthermore, NGA Center/CCSSO are the sole owners and developers of the Common Core State Standards, and Core Common Standards makes no claims to the contrary.

All Graphics, Images, and Logos are © Copyright 2012 CoreCommonStandards.com. Also, the organization of this book and Table of Contents has been created by and organized by CoreCommonStandards.com and HaveFunTeaching.com.

Fore more Common Core Standards Posters, Activities, Worksheets, and Workbooks, visit http://CoreCommonStandards.com.

Worksheets created by: Have Fun Teaching
Activities created by: Have Fun Teaching
Posters created by: Have Fun Teaching

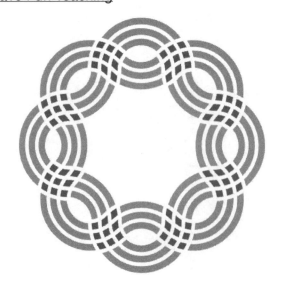

Made in the USA
Monee, IL
08 November 2023

46008857R00087